Flowers, Foreplay, Facelifts Flatulence

A humorous romp through the four stages of relationships

Thomas F. Shubnell

ISBN - 145375945X
EAN - 9781453759455

Cover and interior design by TFS

Autohagiography

If you enjoy this, you will also love, "Gracious Me . . . Is Nothing Sacred." A non-sectarian and hilarious look at all religions from the beginning of time. It truly proves that laughter is good for the soul.

Medical humor abounds in the best selling "Medical Humor" medical nonsense to tickle your funnybone. A great collection of medical funny stuff, including stories, jokes, and hilarious pictures and cartoons.

Another wacky book, "Men vs. Women, a Book of Lists" examines life from a different perspective and tells it all - the differences between the sexes are real and funny.

Speaking of wacky, why not read, "Number One book of Wacky Lists", a hilarious compendium of lists from the sublime to the absurd. Interesting facts and bits of wisdom, humor, and just plain common sense. Something for everyone to enjoy.

Even more fun can be found in "The Best of Terrible Tommy and Yucky Chucky," a collection of the best Terrible Tommy and Yucky Chucky jokes of all time.

More hilarious reading can be found in "Giggles, Gags, and Quips, Special Picks" a collection of the best jokes, pictures, billboards, stories, and cartoons.

Also collect all the "Greatest Jokes of the Century" series of books. 25 wildly funny and hilarious compendiums of the greatest jokes, tidbits, stories, and trivia that are sure to induce uncontrollable laughter. The best bathroom reading since Readers Digest.

Don't forget to collect my Profound Thoughts, a book series of great wisdom, aphorisms, and quotes from great minds.

All written by Thomas F. Shubnell, Ph.D. and available online, your favorite bookstore, or as ebooks.

You might also enjoy my blog at shubsthoughts.blogspot.com

Please ask your local library to carry these books.

Table of Contents

Prologue

This, dear students, is the formula for understanding women.

Adam and Eve

Adam was hanging around the Garden of Eden feeling very lonely.

God asked him, "What's wrong with you?"

Adam said he didn't have anyone to talk to.

God said that He was going to make Adam a companion and that it would be a woman.

He said, "This pretty lady will gather food for you, she will cook for you, and when you discover clothing, she will wash it for you.

She will always agree with every decision you make and she will not nag you and will always be the first to admit she was wrong, when you have had a disagreement.

She will praise you. She will bear your children and never ask you to get up in the middle of the night to take care of them.

She will never have a headache and will freely give you love and passion whenever you need it."

Adam asked God, "What will a woman like this cost?"

God replied, "An arm and a leg."

Then Adam asked, "What can I get for just a rib?"

Of course the rest is history. . .

Idle Thoughts

Life is cruel to men.
When they are born, their mothers get compliments and flowers.
When they get married, their brides get presents and publicity.
When they die, their wives get the sympathy and the insurance money.

The fair sex, as the weaker sex is unfair, since the weaker sex is the stronger sex, because of the weakness of the stronger sex for the weaker sex.

The world is full of men who convert this weakness into a lifelong bondage called marriage. They are perhaps too innocent to realize that marriage is the name of the game where the man loses his bachelor's degree and the woman gets her master's degree.

Different bachelors have different compulsions to walk into this bondage. Those who marry in haste repent in leisure as the better half starts looking like the bitter half.

The joint account is never overdrawn by the wife. It is always under deposited by the husband.

To keep your marriage brimming, with love in the loving cup,
Whenever you're wrong, admit it. Whenever you're right, shut up.

Mutual trust and confidence is critical to marital harmony, as every husband expects himself to be his wife's first love while every wife hopes to be her husband's last.

In the ultimate analysis, marriage turns out to be like a cafeteria. You choose what you like and pay for it later. What you pay and how much you pay depends upon your luck.

Gods Children

After creating Heaven and earth, and Adam and Eve, the first thing God said to them was, "Don't."

"Don't what?" Adam replied.

"Don't eat the forbidden fruit," God said.

"Forbidden fruit? We have forbidden fruit? Hey Eve, we have forbidden fruit."

"No way."

"Yes."

"I told you, don't eat that fruit," said God.

"Why?"

"Because I am your Father and I said so," said God.

A few minutes later God saw his kids having an apple break and was very angry. "Didn't I tell you not to eat the fruit?"

"Uh huh," Adam replied.

"Then why did you?"

"I don't know," Eve answered.

"She started it," Adam said.

"Did not!" "Did too!" "Did not!"

God had enough and His punishment was that Adam and Eve should have children of their own.

Thus the pattern was set for all time and it has never changed. . .

Quotes about Men

I like men to behave like men - strong and childish. Francoise Sagan

A man is like a phonograph with half a dozen records. You soon get tired of them all; and yet you have to sit at the table whilst he reels them off to every new visitor. George Bernard Shaw

A man in love is incomplete until he has married. Then he's finished. Zsa Zsa Gabor

Men are creatures with two legs and eight hands. Jayne Mansfield

Give a man a free hand and he'll run it all over you. Mae West

Husbands never become good; they merely become proficient. H. L. Mencken

The majority of husbands remind me of an orangutan trying to play the violin. Honore de Balzac

A husband is what's left of the lover once the nerve has been extracted. Helen Rowland

Men fantasize about being in bed with two women. Women fantasize about it too because at least they'll have someone to talk to when he falls asleep. Anon

His mother should have thrown him away and kept the stork. Mae West

The husband who wants a happy marriage should learn to keep his mouth shut and his check book open. Groucho Marx

Women have many faults, but men have only two: everything they say, and everything they do. Anon

Quotes about Women

Women are like elephants to me - I like to look at 'em, but I would not want to own one. W. C. Fields

A woman will flirt with anybody in the world as long as other people are looking on. Oscar Wilde

Woman would be more charming if one could fall into her arms without falling into her hands. Ambrose Bierce

Women should be obscene and not heard. Groucho Marx

There's nothing so similar to one poodle dog as another poodle dog, and that goes for women too. Pablo Picasso

I hate women because they always know where things are. James Thurber

Whatever women do they must do twice as well as men to be thought half as good. Luckily this is not difficult. Charlotte Whitton

A woman will always sacrifice herself if you give her the opportunity. It's her favorite form of self-indulgence. W. Somerset Maugham

Never feel remorse for what you have thought about your wife. She has thought much worse things about you. Jean Rostand

Nature intended women to be our slaves ... they are our property; we are not theirs. They belong to us, just as a tree that bears fruit belongs to a gardener. What a mad idea to demand equality for women! Women are nothing but machines for producing children. Napoleon Bonaparte

A woman drove me to drink, and I never even had the courtesy to thank her. W. C. Fields

Friendship

Between Women

A woman didn't come home one night.

The next day she told her husband that she had slept over at a girlfriend's house.

The man called his wife's ten best friends. None of them knew anything about it.

Between Men

A man didn't come home one night.

The next day he told his wife that he had slept over at a buddy's house.

The woman called her husband's ten best friends.

Eight of them confirmed that he had slept over, and two claimed that he was still there.

Just discovered - The original, 'pull my finger' joke

Mating Rituals

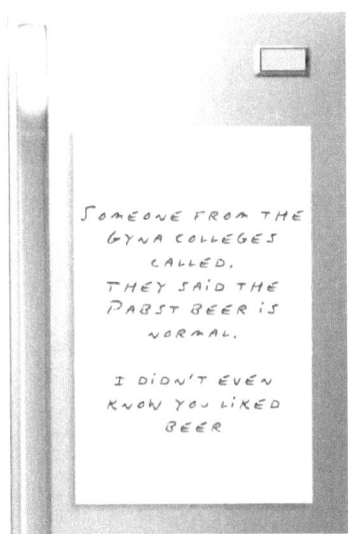

Dating

First Date

A girl asks her boyfriend to come over Friday night and have dinner with her parents. Since this is such a big event, the girl announces to her boyfriend that after dinner, she would like to go out and make love for the first time.

The boy is ecstatic, but he has never had sex before, so he takes a trip to the pharmacist to buy some condoms. The pharmacist helps the boy for about an hour. He tells the boy everything there is to know about condoms and sex.

At the register, the pharmacist asks the boy how many condoms he would like to buy, a three-pack, ten-pack, or family pack. The boy insists on the family pack because he thinks he will be rather busy, because it will be his first time.

That night, the boy shows up at the girl's parent's house and meets his girlfriend at the door. She says, "I am so excited for you to meet my parents, come on in."

He goes inside and is taken to the dinner table where the girl's parents are seated. The boy quickly offers to say grace and bows his head.

A minute passes, and the boy is still deep in prayer, with his head down. Ten minutes pass and still no movement from the boy.

Finally, after twenty minutes with his head down, the girlfriend leans over and whispers to him, "I had no idea you were this religious."

The lad turns, and whispers back, "I had no idea your father was a pharmacist."

Thoughts of Love and Sex

If you want to be loved, you have to be worth loving.

If at first you don't succeed - try a little ardor.

Love is a condition of the mind at a time when the mind is out of condition.

People say that love doesn't last; neither does an ice cream cone, but it's delicious while it does.

Sex takes up the least amount of time and causes the most amount of trouble.

Love doesn't make the world go round. It's what makes the ride worthwhile.

Sex appeal is fifty percent what you have and fifty percent what people think you have.

You can give without loving, but you can't love without giving.

Sex for women is like snow. You never know how many inches you will get or how long it will last.

Never sleep with anyone crazier than yourself.

Qualities that attract a woman to a man are the same ones she can't stand years later.

True love doesn't consist of holding hands - it consists of holding hearts.

Sex is dirty, only if it's done right.

The game of love is never called off because of darkness.

It wasn't the apple on the tree, but the pair on the ground that caused trouble in Eden.

Love is a matter of chemistry. Sex is a matter of physics.

Sex is a three-letter word which needs four-letter words to convey its meaning.

Love is the triumph of imagination over intelligence.

Abstain from wine, women, and song; mostly song.

Never argue with a woman when she is tired, or rested.

A woman never forgets the men she could have had. A man never forgets the women he couldn't.

It is better to be looked over than overlooked.

Love can be divided endlessly and still not diminish.

Love is the delusion that one woman differs from another.

Too many people believe in loss of love at first slight.

In labors of love, every day is payday.

Sexual Marketing

Direct Marketing

You see a gorgeous girl at a party.
You go up to her and say, "I am fantastic in bed."

Telemarketing

You see a gorgeous girl at a party. You go up to her and get her telephone number. The next day you call and say, "Hi, I am fantastic in bed."

Advertising

You're at a party with a bunch of friends and see a gorgeous girl. One of your friends goes up to her and points at you, saying, "He is fantastic in bed."

Public Relations

You're at a party and see a gorgeous girl. You get up and straighten your tie. You walk up to her and pour her a drink. You open the door for her, pick up her bag after she drops it, offer her a ride, and then say, "By the way, I am fantastic in bed."

Brand Recognition

You are at a party and see a gorgeous girl. She walks up to you and says, "I hear you are fantastic in bed."

Date Drugs

Police are warning all clubbers, partygoers, and pub regulars to be alert and stay cautious when offered a drink from any woman.

A new date rape drug on the market called 'beer' is being used by many females to target unsuspecting men. The drug is generally found in liquid form and is available almost anywhere.

'Beer' is used by female sexual predators at parties and bars to persuade their male victims to go home and have sex with them.

Typically, a woman needs only to persuade a man to consume a few units of 'beer' and then simply ask him home for no-strings-attached sex.

Men are rendered helpless against this approach. After several 'beers' men will often succumb to desires to perform sexual acts on horrific looking women to whom they would never normally be attracted.

After drinking 'beer' men often awaken with only hazy memories of exactly what happened to them the night before, often with just a vague feeling that something bad occurred. At other times, these unfortunate men are swindled out of their life's savings in a familiar fraud known as a relationship.

Apparently, men are much more susceptible after 'beer' is administered and sex is performed by the predatory female.

Please pass along this warning to every male you know.

If you fall victim to this insidious 'beer' and the predatory women administering it, there are male support groups in every town, where you can discuss the details of your shocking encounter in an open and frank manner with similarly affected, like-minded guys.

For the support group nearest you, just look up 'Golf Courses' in the yellow pages or on the internet.

Perfect Breasts

Ray Addy is walking down the street and sees a woman with perfect breasts. He says to her, "Hey lady, would you let me bite your breasts for a hundred dollars?"

"Are you crazy?" she replies and walks away.

He turns around, runs around the block, and gets to the corner before she does.

"Would you let me bite your breasts for a thousand dollars?" Ray asks.

"Listen sir, I'm not that kind of woman."

So Ray runs around the next block and faces her again, "Would you let me bite your breasts for ten thousand dollars?"

She thinks about it for a while and says, "Hmm, ten thousand dollars, eh? OK, but not here. Let's go to that dark alley over there."

They go over to the alley and she takes off the blouse to reveal the most perfect breasts in the world.

As soon as Ray sees them he grabs them and starts caressing them, fondling them, kissing them, licking them, and burying his face in them, but no biting.

After a while, the woman gets annoyed and asks, "Are you going to bite them, eh?"

"Nah," Ray replies, "Too expensive."

Doctor Date

One night, a man and a woman are at a bar downing a few beers. They strike up a conversation and quickly discover that they're both doctors.

After about an hour, the man says to the woman, "How would you like to come back to my place and sleep with me tonight? No strings attached. It will just be one night of fun."

The woman agrees and they go back to his place. She goes into the bathroom and starts scrubbing up like she's about to go into the operating room. She scrubs for what seems like ten to twenty minutes.

Finally, she comes into the bedroom and they have sex for a very long time.

Afterwards, the man says to the woman, "You're a surgeon, aren't you?"

"Yes, how did you know?"

"I could tell by the way you scrubbed up before we started."

"Oh, that makes sense," says the woman.

"You're an anesthesiologist, aren't you?"

"Yes I am," says the man. "How did you know?"

The woman replies, "I didn't feel a thing."

Girlfriend Software

I'm currently running the latest version of GirlFriend and I have been having some problems lately. I have been running the same version of DrinkingBuddies forever as my primary application, and all the GirlFriend releases I tried have always conflicted with it.

I hear that DrinkingBuddies 1.0 won't crash if GirlFriend is run in background mode and the sound is turned off, but am embarrassed to say I can't find the switch to turn the sound off. I just run them separately and it works okay. Girlfriend also seems to have a problem co-existing with my Golf program, often trying to abort Golf with some sort of timing incompatibility.

I probably should have stayed with GirlFriend 1.0, but I thought I might see better performance from GirlFriend 2.0. After months of conflicts and other problems, I consulted a friend who has had experience with GirlFriend 2.0. He said I probably didn't have enough cache to run GirlFriend 2.0, and eventually it would require a Token Ring to run properly. He was right. As soon as I purged my cache, it uninstalled itself.

Shortly after that, I installed GirlFriend 3.0 beta. All the bugs were supposed to be gone, but the first time I used it, it gave me a virus anyway. I had to clean out my whole system and shut down for a while.

I very cautiously upgraded to GirlFriend 4.0. This time I used a SCSI probe first and also installed a virus protection program. It worked okay for a while until I discovered that GirlFriend 1.0 was still in my system. I tried running GirlFriend 1.0 again with GirlFriend 4.0 still installed, but GirlFriend 4.0 has a feature I didn't know about that automatically senses the presence of any other version of GirlFriend and communicates with it in some way, which results in the immediate removal of both versions.

The version I have now works pretty well, but there are still some problems. Like all versions of GirlFriend, it is written in some obscure language I can't understand, much less reprogram.

Frankly I think there is too much attention paid to the look and feel rather than the desired functionality.

Also, to get the best connections with your hardware, you usually have to use gold-plated contacts, and I have never liked how GirlFriend is totally object-oriented.

A year ago, a friend of mine upgraded his version of GirlFriend to GirlFriendPlus 1.0, which is a Terminate and Stay Resident version of GirlFriend. He discovered that GirlFriendPlus 1.0 expires within a year if you don't upgrade to Fiancee 1.0. So he did, but soon after that, he had to upgrade to Wife 1.0, which is a huge resource hog. It has taken up all his space, so he can't load anything else.

One of the primary reasons he decided to go with Wife 1.0 was because it came bundled with FreeSexPlus. It turns out the resource allocation module of Wife 1.0 sometimes prohibits access to FreeSexPlus, particularly the new Plug-Ins he wanted to try. In addition, Wife 1.0 must be running on a well warmed-up system before he can do anything.

Although he did not ask for it, Wife 1.0 came with Mother-in-Law which has an automatic pop-up feature he can't turn off. I told him to try installing Mistress 1.0, but he said he heard if you try to run it without first uninstalling Wife 1.0, Wife 1.0 will delete MSMoney files before doing the uninstall itself. Then Mistress 1.0 won't install because of insufficient resources.

Beautiful Ears

Bob Saluzzo rents an apartment in New York, and goes to the lobby to put his name on his new mailbox. While there, an attractive young lady comes out of the apartment next to the mailboxes wearing a silk robe.

He smiles at the young girl and she begins a conversation with him. As they talk, her robe slips open, and it's quite obvious that she has nothing under the robe.

Bob breaks into a sweat trying to maintain eye contact. After a few minutes, she places her hand on his arm and says, "Let's go in my apartment, I think I hear someone coming."

He proceeds with her into the apartment, and after she closes the door, she leans against it allowing her robe to fall off completely.

Being completely nude, she purrs at him, "What would you say is my best feature?"

Bob is completely flustered, stammers, clears his throat several times, and finally says, "Oh, it has to be your ears."

She asks, "Why do you say my ears? Looks at these breasts, they are full, don't sag, and they are all natural. My buns are firm and have no cellulite. Look at this skin, no blemishes, or scars. Why in heaven's name would you say my ears are the best part of my body?"

Clearing his throat once again, Bob stammers, "Outside when you said you heard someone coming, it was me."

Dear John

The importance of proper punctuation can be found in these two 'Dear John' letters. *Further proof below the second letter.*

Dear John,

I want a man who knows what love is all about. You are generous, kind, thoughtful. People who are not like you admit to being useless and inferior.

You have ruined me for other men. I yearn for you. I have no feelings whatsoever when we are apart. I can be forever happy; will you let me be yours?

Marge

Version Two

Dear John,

I want a man who knows what love is. All about you are generous, kind, thoughtful people, who are not like you. Admit to being useless and inferior.

You have ruined me. For other men, I yearn. For you, I have no feelings whatsoever. When we are apart, I can be forever happy. Will you let me be?

Marge

More Proof

A woman without her man is nothing

Male version: A woman, without her man, is nothing.

Female Version: A woman: without her, man is nothing.

Fast Watch

A rather confident man walks into a bar and takes a seat next to a very attractive woman. He gives her a quick glance, and then casually looks at his watch for a moment.

The woman notices this and asks, "Is your date running late?"

"No," he replies, "I just bought this state-of-the-art watch and I was just testing it."

The intrigued woman says, "A state-of-the-art watch? What's so special about it?"

"It uses alpha waves to telepathically talk to me," he explains.

"What's it telling you now?"

"It says you are not wearing any panties."

The woman giggles and replies, "It must be broken, because I am wearing panties."

The man says, "Damn thing must be an hour fast."

Husband Shopping

There is a Husband Shopping Center where a woman can go to select a husband.

It is laid out in five floors, with the men increasing in positive attributes as you ascend up the floors. The only rule is, once you open the door to any floor, you must choose a man from that floor, and if you go up a floor, you can't go back down except to leave.

Two girlfriends go to find a prospective husband.

First floor door sign: "These men have jobs and love kids."

The women read the sign and say, "That's better than not having jobs, or not loving kids, but I wonder what's further up."

They go up another floor.

Second floor sign: "These men have high paying jobs, love kids, and are extremely good looking"

The girls wonder what could be further up.

Third floor sign: "These men have high paying jobs, are extremely good looking, love kids, and help with the housework."

"Very tempting, but there's more, further up." Up they go.

Fourth floor sign: "These men have high paying jobs, love kids, are extremely good looking, help with the housework, and have a strong romantic streak."

"Almost perfect, but just think what must be awaiting us further up."

Up to the fifth floor they go. The sign on the door: "This floor is just to prove that women are impossible to please."

Disease

A guy picked up a girl at a local dance. After they danced, he said, "I would take you to my house, but my parents are home."

The woman replied, "I would let you come to my house, except my boyfriend is staying there."

The guy suggested that they go to his van.

She agreed and they went to the van. They both took off their clothes, and at the point where the man was about to enter her, she exclaimed, "What, no foreplay? How about going outside and look for a stick, and you can beat me with it."

The man went outside, but couldn't find any sticks. So instead he busted the aerial off his van and the guy and girl beat each other on the back and they had a great evening time.

The next morning, the man was feeling very sore from all of the hits that had received on his back.

He went to his doctor, who exclaimed, "This is the worst case of Van-Aerial disease I have ever seen."

Dress for the Occasion

Barbara and Suzie are having a conversation.

Barbara begins by saying, "That nice Paul asked me out for a date. I know you went out with him last week, and I wanted to talk with you about him before I give him my answer."

Suzie responds, "He showed up at my apartment punctually at seven. He was dressed like a gentleman in a fine suit and he brought me beautiful flowers.

Then, he took me downstairs, where I saw a limousine with a uniformed chauffeur. He took me out for a marvelous dinner of lobster, champagne, dessert, and after dinner drinks.

After dinner, we went to see a show. Let me tell you Barbara, I enjoyed it so much I could have just died from the pleasure.

When the show ended, we came back to my apartment and he turned into an animal. Completely crazy, he tore off my expensive new dress, and had his way with me twice."

Barbara exclaims, "Goodness gracious. So, are you are telling me I should not go out with him?"

Suzie replies, "No, I'm just trying to tell you to wear an old dress."

Breakup Letter

Dear _____,

I regret to inform you that you have been eliminated from further contention as Mr. Right. As you are probably aware, the competition was exceedingly tough and dozens of well-qualified candidates such as yourself also failed to make the final cut. I will, however, keep your name on file should an opening come available. So that you may find better success in your future romantic endeavors, please allow me to offer the following reason(s) you were disqualified from the competition: (Check those that apply)

Your last name is objectionable. I can't imagine taking it, hyphenating it, or subjecting my children to it.

Your first name is objectionable. It's just not something I can picture myself yelling out in a fit of passion.

The fact that our finest dining experience to date has been at McDonald's reveals a thriftiness that I find unappealing.

Your inadvertent admission that you 'buy condoms by the truckload' indicates that you may be interested in me for something other than my personality.

You failed the 20 Question Rule, i.e., I asked you 20 questions about yourself before you asked me more than one about myself.

Your breasts are bigger than mine.

Your legs are skinnier than mine. If you can FIT into my pants, then you can't GET into my pants.

You are too short. Any son that we produced would inevitably be beaten up repeatedly at recess.

You are too tall. I am developing a chronic neck condition from trying to kiss you.

The fact that your apartment has been condemned reveals an inherent slovenliness that I fear is unbreakable.

Although I do enjoy the X-Files, I find your wardrobe of Star Trek uniforms a little disconcerting.

Your frequent references to your ex-girlfriend lead me to suspect that you are some sort of psychotic stalker.

Your ability to belch the alphabet is not a trait that I am seeking in a long term partner.

Your height is out of proportion to your weight. If you should, however, happen to gain the necessary 17 vertical inches, please resubmit your application.

The fact that you categorize the Pro Bowler's Tour as 'Must See TV' demonstrated that you do not meet my intelligence requirements.

Somehow I doubt those condoms that I found in your overnight bag were really necessary for a successful business trip.

I am out of your league; set your sights lower next time.

Sincerely, _____

Harley Love

A guy has always dreamed of owning a Harley Davidson. One day he has finally saved up enough money so he goes down to the dealer. After he picks out the perfect bike, the dealer tells him about an old biker trick that will keep the chrome on his new bike free from rust.

The dealer tells him to keep a jar of Vaseline handy and put it on the chrome before it rains, and everything will be fine. He happily pays for the bike and leaves.

A few months later, the young man meets a woman and falls in love. She asks him to meet her parents for dinner. He readily accepts and the date is set. At the appointed time, he picks her up on his Harley and they ride to her parent's house.

Before they go in, she tells him that they have a family tradition that whoever speaks first after dinner must do the dishes. After a delicious dinner everyone sits in silence waiting for the first person to break the silence and get stuck doing the dishes.

After a long fifteen minutes, the young man decides to speed things up, so he reaches over and kisses his girl in front of her family. No one says a word.

He then slips his hand under her blouse and fondles her breasts. Still no one says a word. Finally, he throws her on the table and has sex with her in front of everyone. No one says a word.

Now he is getting desperate, so he grabs her mother and throws her on the table. They have even wilder sex. Still no one speaks.

By now he is thinking what to do next when he hears thunder in the distance. His first thought is to protect the chrome on his Harley, so he gets his jacket, reaches in his pocket, and pulls out his jar of Vaseline.

Her father says, "OK, I'll do the dishes."

Good Job

Nick met a beautiful girl in a local pub, took her out to dinner and dancing, and showed her an excellent time.

When she asked what he did for a living, he replied that he was a sanitation executive for the city.

A few days later she was walking down the street and she happened to see someone that looked as if it might be Nick down at the bottom of a manhole. She looked closer and realized that it was indeed him.

He was scooping sludge at the bottom of the hole and handing it to the man above him who, in turn, was handing it to the man above him, who was handing it to the man in the street, who was dumping it into the back of a city truck.

She yelled down, "Nick, I thought that you told me that you were a sanitation executive?"

He looked up at her from the hole and replied, "I am. You don't see anyone handing me any shit, do you?"

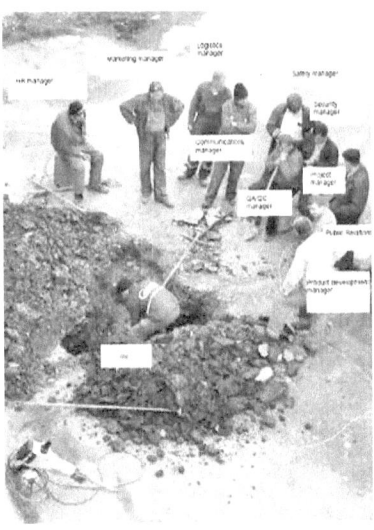

41

Erection Control

Phil walks into a bar and sees his friend Jim slumped over the bar. He walks over and asks Jim what's wrong.

"Well," replies Jim, "You know that beautiful girl at work that I wanted to ask out, but I got an erection every time I saw her?"

"Yes," replies Phil with a laugh.

Jim says, "Well, I finally worked up the courage to ask her out, and she agreed."

"That's great," says Phil, "When are you going out?"

"I went to meet her this evening, but I was worried I would get an erection again. So I got some duct tape and taped my thingie to my leg, so if I got a woody, it wouldn't show."

"Sensible," says Phil.

"So I get to her door, and rang her doorbell. She answered it in the sheerest, sexiest, dress you ever saw."

"And what happened then?"

"It grew, my leg straightened with it, and I kicked her in the face."

Drinking Limit

A guy walks into a bar and notices a beautiful woman sitting at a table. He strolls over to her and says, "You know, I would love to kiss your boobs."

The woman says, "My boyfriend is the bouncer here, and if you don't leave me alone I'll have him punch you."

"Ok, I'm sorry," says the guy as he buys another drink.

After a few more drinks the guy walks over to her again and says, "You know, I would love to kiss you on your butt."

The woman is very angry and says, "One more word from you and I'm going to get my boyfriend."

"Ok, I'm sorry. It won't happen again," says the guy.

A few more and the guy is totally drunk. He approaches the woman, "I would love to fill up your snatch with beer and drink it out."

"That does it, I'm getting my boyfriend. You are in so much trouble." The woman goes to the backroom, and tells her boyfriend what happened. "There is a man out there who said that he wants to kiss my breasts." Her boyfriend stands up and rolls up his shirt sleeves. "And, he said that he wanted to kiss my butt." Clenching his fists, he reaches for his baseball bat.

"He also says he wants to fill my snatch with beer and drink every bit of it out of there."

Hearing this, the boyfriends face turns white, breaks out in a sweat, and sits down.

The woman is shocked and asks, "Hey, aren't you going to take care of him?"

"Heck no," says the boyfriend. "I am not going to mess with anyone that can drink that much."

Meeting His Family

A woman goes to her boyfriend's parent's house for dinner. This is to be her first time meeting the family and she is very nervous. They all sit down and begin eating a fine meal.

The woman is beginning to feel a little discomfort, thanks to her nervousness and the broccoli casserole. The gas pains are almost making her eyes water. Left with no other choice, she decides to relieve herself a bit and lets out a dainty little fart. It wasn't loud, but everyone at the table heard the toot.

Before she even had a chance to be embarrassed, her boyfriend's father looked over at the dog that had been snoozing at the woman's feet, and said in a rather stern voice, "Ginger!"

The woman thought that was great and a big smile came across her face. A couple minutes later, she was beginning to feel the pain again. This time, she didn't even hesitate. She let a much louder and longer fart rip.

The father again looked at the dog and yelled, "Dammit Ginger!"

Again the woman smiled and thought it was super. A few minutes later the woman had to let another one rip.

This time she didn't even think about it. She let rip with a fart that rivaled a train whistle blowing.

Again, the father looked at the dog with disgust and yelled, "Dammit Ginger, get away from that girl before she craps on you."

Small Parts

A rather flat-chested young lady went to Doctor Ace for advice about enlarging her breasts.

He told her, "Everyday when you get out of the shower, rub your nipples and say, "Scooby doobie doobies, I want bigger boobies."

She did this faithfully for several months, and it worked. She grew larger boobs.

One morning she was running late and when she was on the bus she realized she had forgotten her morning ritual. At this point she loved her new boobs and didn't want to lose them. So she got up, right in the middle of the bus, and said, "Scooby doobie doobies, I want bigger boobies."

A guy was sitting nearby and asked her, "Do you go to Doctor Ace by any chance?"

"Why yes, I do. How did you know?"

He leaned toward her and whispered, "Hickory Dickory Dock."

Size Matters

A male elf was so paranoid about the miniature size of his thingie that he could never work up the courage to have sex. Then one day he fell in love with an elf nurse.

One fine evening, they went back to her place. She put on some soft music and led him into the bedroom.

Totally mortified, he told her of his problem.

"Don't worry," She said. "I'm a nurse. I won't laugh."

The embarrassed elf drops his trousers.

"It's OK," she said. "I've seen lots smaller than that."

"Really?" the relieved elf asked.

She nodded and replied, "Yes, I used to work in a maternity ward."

Buying Gifts

Darren decided to buy his new girlfriend a birthday present and after much thought, he chose a pair of gloves. He went with a friend to the mall and his friend bought a pair of lace panties for his wife. They had the gifts wrapped and delivered to their respective homes.

Somehow the packages were mixed up and his girlfriend received the panties and his friend's wife received the gloves.

Darren had carefully written a note to accompany the gloves and asked that it be attached to the gift for delivery.

Monique,

This little gift is to show you that I have not forgotten your birthday. I chose this gift for you because I noticed that you are not in the habit of wearing any when we go out. A friend suggested that I choose longer ones, but I know that the shorter ones are in fashion now.

I know that they appear to be very delicate, but the lady at the counter showed me a pair that she had been wearing for a few weeks and you could not notice any soiling whatever. I had her try on this pair and they looked especially good on her. She suggested that you blow into them when you take them off as they will probably be a bit damp from wearing.

I only hope no other hands will touch them before we go out again and that you will wear them for me on our next date. I also hope the size is correct as I am usually a good judge of these things. I can hardly wait to kiss them when we meet.

Love, Darren

P. S. The shop girl showed me the best way to wear them is unbuttoned and hanging down.

Following Her

A man was playing on the front nine of a complicated golf layout and became confused as to where he was on the course. He looked around and saw a lady playing ahead of him, so he walked up to her, explained his confusion, and asked her if she knew what hole he was playing.

She replied, "I am on the seventh hole, and you are a hole behind me, so you must be on the sixth hole."

He thanked her and went back to his golf.

On the back nine the same thing happened and he approached her again with the same request.

She said, "I'm on the fourteenth hole, you are a hole behind me, so you must be on the thirteenth hole."

Once again he thanked her and returned to his play.

He finished his round and went to the clubhouse where he saw the same lady sitting at the bar. He asked the bartender if he knew her. The bartender said she was a sales lady and played the course often.

He approached her and said, "Let me buy you a drink in appreciation for your help. I understand that you are in the sales profession. I'm in sales, also. What do you sell?"

She replied, "If I tell you, you'll laugh." "No, I won't."

"If you must know," she answered, "I work for 'Tampax'."

He laughed so hard, he almost lost his breath.

She said, "See I knew you would laugh."

He replied, "That's not what I'm laughing at. I'm a salesman for 'Preparation H', so I am still a hole behind you."

Prescriptions

Paul is ninety-two and Amy is eighty-five. They are all excited about their decision to get married.

They go for a stroll to discuss the wedding and on the way go past a drugstore. Amy suggests that they go in. She addresses the man behind the counter and says, "Are you the owner?"

The pharmacist answers, "Yes."

Amy, "Do you sell heart medication?"

Pharmacist, "Of course we do."

Amy, "How about medicine for circulation?"

Pharmacist, "All kinds."

Amy, "Medicine for rheumatism?"

Pharmacist, "Definitely."

Amy, "How about Viagra?"

Pharmacist, "Of course."

Amy, "Medicine for memory?"

Pharmacist, "Yes, a large variety."

Amy, "What about vitamins and sleeping pills?"

Pharmacist, "Absolutely."

Amy turns to Paul and says, "Sweetheart, we should register our wedding gift list at this store."

Marriage Choices

A wealthy young man's parents told him he must be married by his twenty-fifth birthday in order to fulfill the terms of their joint will and get the money. This was a bit of a dilemma to him because he was dating three lovely young ladies and couldn't decide.

As he had only one month, he came up with a plan. He gave each woman five thousand dollars and told her she had a month to spend it, and, she could spend it any way she wanted.

After the month he met with each.

The first one said, "You know I love to shop, so I spent all of it on clothes."

"Fair enough," he replied, and made note of her decision.

The second young woman said, "I think it's better to give than receive, so I gave all of my money to charity."

"Fine," said the young man.

Number three said, "You know I have a mind for saving, so I invested it in ten percent zero coupon treasury bonds."

"Interesting," replied the gentleman, smiling at her keen financial acumen.

So, which one did he choose?

The one with big boobs, of course.

Sportsman's Double

A guy had an interesting experience recently involving an older woman he met at a bar.

She looked pretty darn hot for sixty. She was drinking quite a bit and, while they were chatting, she came right out and asked him if he ever had a 'sportsman's double', a mother and daughter threesome.

He told her no, but she might be able to talk him into it.

She slams back one last drink, wipes her mouth, and looks directly into his eyes and says, "Tonight is your lucky night."

So they go back to her place. She clicks on the hall light as they enter her place, and she shouts upstairs, "Mom, are you still awake?"

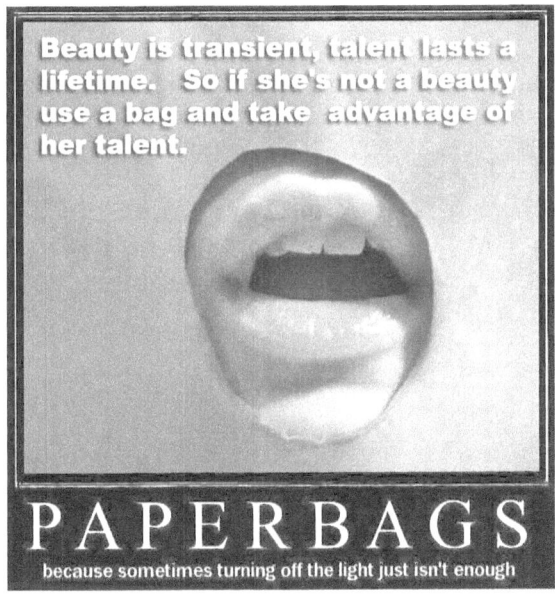

Accidents Happen

On their way to get married, a young couple was involved in a fatal car accident. The couple found themselves sitting outside the Pearly Gates waiting for Saint Peter to process them into Heaven.

While waiting, they wondered if they could possibly get married in Heaven. When Saint Peter showed up, they asked him.

Saint Peter replied, "I don't know. This is the first time anyone has asked. Let me go find out." He went away. The couple sat there and waited for an answer for a couple of months.

While they waited, they discussed that if they were allowed to get married in Heaven, and if it didn't work out, would they be stuck together forever?

Finally, after several months Saint Peter returned. "Yes," he informed the couple, "You can get married in Heaven."

"Great!" said the couple, "But we were wondering, if things didn't work out, could we get divorced in Heaven?"

Saint Peter was red-faced with anger and slams his clipboard down.

"What's wrong?" asked the frightened couple.

Saint Peter sputters, "It took me three months to find a priest up here. Do you have any idea how long it will take me to find a lawyer?"

Kingly Gifts

The beautiful secretary of a bank president goes on a sightseeing tour with a very rich African king who was a very important client. The client, out of the blue, asks her to marry him. Naturally, the secretary is quite surprised. However, she remembers that her boss told her not to reject the guy outright, so, she tries to think of a way to dissuade the king from wanting to marry her.

After a few minutes, the woman says to the man, "I will only marry you under three conditions. First, I want my engagement ring to be a 75-carat diamond ring with a matching 200-carat diamond tiara."

The African king pauses for awhile. Then he nods his head and says, "No problem! I do it. I do it."

The woman thought this was too easy and says to the man, "I want you to build me a 100-room mansion in New York. And as a vacation home, I want a chateau built in the middle of the best wine country in France."

The African king pauses for awhile. He whips out his cellular phone and calls some brokers in New York and in France. He looks at the woman, nods his head, and says, "OK, OK. I build. I build."

She now has one last condition. She knows that she better make this a good one. She takes her time to think and finally she gets an idea, a sure thing condition. She squints her eyes, looks at the man and says, "Since I like sex, I want the man I marry to have a 14-inch penis."

The man appears a bit disturbed. He cups his face with his hands and rests his elbows on the table, all the while muttering in African dialect.

Finally, after what seems like forever, the king shakes his head, looking very sad, and says to the woman, "OK, OK. I cut. I cut."

Fatherly Advice

It's 1956 and Ray goes to pick up his date, Mary Marcia. Ray's a pretty hip guy with his own car and a ducktail hairdo. When he goes to the front door, Mary Marcia's father answers and invites him in.

"Mary Marcia's not ready yet, so why don't you have a seat?"

Ray says, "That's cool."

Mary Marcia's father asks Ray what they are planning to do. Ray replies politely that they will probably just go to the malt shop or to a drive-in-movie.

Mary Marcia's father responds, "Why don't you kids go out and screw? I hear all of the kids are doing it."

Naturally this comes as quite a surprise to Ray and he says, "What?"

"Yeah," says Mary Marcia's father, "We know that Mary Marcia really likes to screw. She would screw all night if we let her."

Ray's eyes light up and he smiles from ear to ear. Immediately, he has revised the plans for the evening. A few minutes later, Mary Marcia comes downstairs in her little poodle skirt with her saddle shoes and announces that she is ready to go.

Almost breathless with anticipation, Ray escorts his date out the front door while dad is saying, "Have good evening kids." He shoots a small wink at Ray.

About twenty minutes later, a thoroughly disheveled Mary Marcia rushes back into the house, slams the door behind her and screams at her father, "Geez dad, the Twist, it's called the Twist!"

Playing Games

A blonde calls her boyfriend and says, "Please come over here and help me. I have a killer jigsaw puzzle, and I can't figure out how to get it started."

Her boyfriend asks, "What is it supposed to be when it's finished?"

The blonde says, "According to the picture on the box, it's a tiger."

Her boyfriend decides to go over and help with the puzzle.

She lets him in and shows him where she has the puzzle spread all over the table.

He studies the pieces for a moment, then looks at the box, then turns to her and says, "No matter what we do, we are not going to be able to assemble these pieces into anything resembling a tiger."

Then he held her hand and said, "Let's have a cup of coffee, and then we will put all these Frosted Flakes back in the box."

Mean Things

A woman can say to a naked man

I've smoked fatter joints than that.

Are you cold?

Awww, it's so cute.

You know they have surgery to fix that.

Wow, and your feet are so big.

Will it squeak if I squeeze it?

Can I be honest with you?

This explains your car.

Maybe if we water it, it will grow.

At least this won't take long.

I never saw one like that before.

But it still works, right?

It looks so. . . unused.

Maybe it looks better in natural light.

I guess this makes me the early bird.

Proposal

Three men, Myron the lawyer, Kenny the teamster, and Jimmy the Aggie, proposed marriage to an eligible young lady.

Mary couldn't decide which proposal to accept. Myron had a prestigious job, Kenny was a manly man, and Jimmy was very rich.

She told them, "We'll have a contest. I will marry whoever brings me the most ping pong balls."

A couple of days later, Myron came back with an attaché case full of ping pong balls. "Would you please marry me, please?" Myron begged.

Mary was about to accede to Myron when they heard a rumble outside.

Kenny huffed into Mary's apartment and threw open the curtain. On the lawn, were his buddies unloading crate after crate of ping pong balls from a huge truck. Kenny said, "Why don't you marry me right now?"

Mary was pleasantly surprised and told Kenny, "It looks like it's going to be you and me, but I want to be fair. We have to wait for Jimmy."

It was a long wait, but several days later, Jimmy showed up. His clothes were in rags, his body was a mass of cuts and bruises, and he was carrying two huge round objects on his shoulders.

"What happened to you?" Mary asked him. "I waited all this time and you didn't even bring me any ping pong balls."

"Ping pong balls?" said Jimmy, "I thought you said King Kong's balls."

Fixing Problems

A man with a twenty-five inch long penis goes to his doctor to complain that he is having a problem with this cumbersome instrument and has had more than one complaint.

"Doctor, is there anything you can do for me?"

The doctor replies, "Medically son, there is nothing I can do, but I do know this witch who may be able to help you." The doctor gives him directions to the witch.

The man calls upon the witch and relates his story, "Witch, my penis is twenty-five inches long and I need help. Can anything be done to help me? You are my only hope."

The witch stares in amazement, scratches her head, and then replies, "I think I may be able to help you with your problem. Go deep into the forest. You will find a pond with a frog sitting on a log. This frog has magic. Say to the frog, 'will you marry me'? When the frog says no, you will find five inches less to your problem."

The man's face lit up and he dashed off into the forest and called out to the frog, "Will you marry me?" The frog looked at him and replied, "No."

The man looked down and suddenly his penis was five inches shorter. "Wow, this is great." However, it was still too long at twenty inches, so he asked the frog to marry him again. The frog rolled its eyes back and screamed back, "No."

The man felt another twitch in his penis, looked down, and it was another five inches shorter. He thought, just a little less would be ideal. Grinning, he looked across the pond and yelled out, "Frog, will you marry me?"

The frog looked back at him and said, "How many times do I have to tell you? No, No, No."

Instructions for Women

Never do housework. No man ever made love to a woman because the house was spotless.

Don't imagine you can change a man - unless he is in diapers.

So many men - so many reasons not to sleep with any of them.

If they can put a man on the moon - they should be able to put them all there.

Tell him you are not his type - you have a pulse.

Never let your man's mind wander - it's too little to be left out alone.

Never marry a man for money. You'll have to earn every penny.

A bachelor is a man who has missed the opportunity to make some woman miserable.

The best way to get a man to do something is to suggest he is too old for it.

If he asks what sort of books you are interested in, tell him check books.

A man's idea of serious commitment is usually, "OK, I'll stay the night".

Remember a sense of humor does not mean that you tell him jokes; it means you laugh at his.

If he asks you if you are faking it tell him no, you are just practicing.

Doing It

A couple had been dating for some time. Finally they decided it was time for marriage.

Before the wedding, they went out to dinner and had a long conversation regarding how their marriage might work.

They discussed finances, living arrangements, furniture, appliances, and the usual household matters.

Finally the gentleman decided it was time to broach the subject of their physical relationship.

He conjured up all of his courage and leaned toward her and asked, "How do you feel about sex?"

She responding slowly and carefully, "I hadn't considered it, but I would have to say that I would like it infrequently."

The man sat quietly for a moment. Then he looked her in the eye and asked, "Was that one word or two?"

Legal Age

A policeman was patrolling a local parking spot that overlooked a golf course. He drove by and noticed a couple inside a car with the interior dome light on.

In the driver's seat there was a young man reading a computer magazine, while in the backseat was a young woman knitting.

The officer walked up to the driver's window and tapped on the glass, asking the man his name and what he was doing.

The man looked up, cranked the window down, and said, "My name is Ray and that is my girlfriend in the back seat."

"So what are you doing?" asked the officer.

"What does it look like? I'm reading a magazine."

Pointing towards the young lady in the back seat, the officer asked, "And what is she doing?"

Ray looked over his shoulder and replied, "What does it look like? She is knitting, sir."

"And how old are you?" the officer asked.

"I'm twenty five," Ray replied.

"And how old is she?" asked the officer.

Ray looked at his watch and said, "Well sir, in twelve minutes she will be eighteen."

Speak Clearly

Once upon a time there was a Prince who was cast under a spell by an evil witch. The curse was that the Prince could speak only one word each year. However, he could save up the words so that if he did not speak for a whole year, then the following year he was allowed to speak two words.

One day he met a beautiful princess with ruby lips, golden hair, and sapphire eyes, and fell madly in love. With the greatest difficulty he decided to refrain from speaking for two whole years so that he could look at her and say, "My darling."

At the end of the second year he wished to tell her that he loved her, but because of this he waited three more years without speaking.

At the end of these five years he realized that he had to ask her to marry him, so he waited another four years without speaking.

Finally as the ninth year of silence ended, his joy knew no bounds. Leading the lovely princess to the most secluded and romantic place in that beautiful royal garden the prince heaped a hundred red roses on her lap, knelt before her, and taking her hand in his, said huskily, "My darling, I love you. Will you marry me?"

The princess tucked a strand of golden hair behind a dainty ear, opened her sapphire eyes, and parting her lips said, "What did you say?"

Mating Quickies

Men have two emotions, hungry and horny. If you see him without an erection, make him a sandwich.

A British technology company has developed a computer chip that will allow women to store music in their breasts.

Seems like this is a major breakthrough, since women often complain about men who stare at their breasts, but don't listen to them.

One day, Marcia goes up to Ray and asks for twenty dollars to buy meat.

"Are you crazy?" says Ray, who pulls her over to a mirror. "Let me show you something? This twenty-dollar bill is mine. The one in the mirror is yours. Get it?" Marcia nods.

The next day, he returns home to find a freezer full of meat. He is angry, and asks Marcia about it.

She pulls him over to the mirror and lifts up her skirt. "See the one in the mirror? That's yours. This one is the butcher's."

What's the difference between a girlfriend and wife?
Fifty pounds.

Sex is not the answer, sex is the question. Yes is the answer.

Gift wrapping is a woman's idea. If it had been a man's idea, we would just spray paint the box.

A guy and this girl want to have sex, so they go to the girl's house, but before entering her room, the girl stops and says, "My little sister sleeps on the bottom bunk of our bed and I do not want her to knowing what we are doing. So when I say, 'Baloney,' it means push harder, and when I say, 'Pastrami,' it means push softer."

With this, the two get onto the top bunk and have sex. First, the girl moans, "Baloney! Baloney! Baloney!"

Then, she shouts, "Pastrami! Pastrami! Pastrami!" Then, she changes back to, "Baloney! Baloney! Baloney!"

Finally, the girl's sister yells, "Will you quit making sandwiches up there? I'm covered in mayonnaise."

Courting hasn't changed much in 2,000 years; ancient Greek women used to sit around all evening and listen to a lyre, too.

Girl, to mother, "My boyfriend boasts to everyone that he is going to marry the most beautiful girl in the world."
Mother, "Oh that's a shame. I thought he liked you."

Ask any man, and he will tell you that any woman's ultimate fantasy is to have two men at once. While this has been verified by a recent sociological study, it appears that most men do not realize that in this fantasy, one man is cooking and the other is cleaning.

A woman picks up the phone to hear, "Oh darling, I have changed my mind. You can have the Rolls for a wedding present and we can move to any island retreat that your heart desires. We will build a house big enough so you can have your mother stay with us. Now, will you marry me?"

She replied, "Of course I will darling, and who is this speaking?"

Women are like guns, keep one around long enough and you are going to want to shoot it.

Did you hear about the two bedbugs that fell in love?
They got married in the spring.

The blind date was a fiasco from the start, but the guy was too insensitive and ego-ridden to realize it. The moment of truth came at the end of the evening as the guy clutched the girl's thigh and whispered, "How about coming to my place so I can slip you nine inches?"

There was a moment of silence, and then the girl replied, "You know, I really don't think you could get it up three times in a row!"

Do you know what is better than Four Roses on your piano?
Two lips on your organ.

Terrible Tommy and his grandfather go fishing one day. While fishing, the old man starts talking about how times have changed. Tommy picks up on this and starts talking about the various problems and diseases going around.

Tommy says, "Grandpa, they didn't have a whole lot of problems with all these diseases when you were young, did they?"

Grandpa replies, "Nope."

Tommy says, "Well, what did you guys use for safe sex?"

Grandpa replies, "A wedding ring."

How do you get a fat women to go to bed with you"
It's a piece of cake.

Never argue with a woman when she is tired. . . or rested.

A nurse is walking down a hospital corridor when her supervisor spots her.

The supervisor is amazed. The nurse has unkempt hair, her dress is wrinkled, and one of her boobs is hanging out of the front of her uniform.

The Nursing Supervisor asks, "Nurse Smith, how do you account for standard of dress?"

"Oh," says the nurse, as she pushes her boobs back into her uniform. "You know what doctors are like. They never put anything back where they find it."

Whether a man winds up with a nest egg, or a goose egg, depends a lot on the kind of chick he marries.

A guy goes into a bar where he sees a smartly dressed woman perched on a bar stool. He walks up behind her and says, "Hi there, good looking, how's it going?"

She turns around, faces him, looks him straight in the eye and says, "Listen, I will screw anybody, anytime, anywhere, your place, my place, it doesn't matter. I have been doing it ever since I got out of college. I just flat out love it."

"No kidding?" said the man. "I'm a lawyer, too. What firm are you with?"

My girlfriend says that she would rather be raped by Jack the Ripper than fingered by Captain Hook.

Tom and Sherri were lying in bed one night. Sherri was curled up, ready to go to sleep and Tom was reading a book.

Periodically, he would fondle her 'special area' for a few seconds, wait a minute or so, and then fondle her again.

Sherri gradually became aroused and soon started rubbing him back.

"What are you doing?" Tom asked.

She replied, "You were rubbing me downtown. Don't you want to do it?"

"No, not tonight."

"Then what the hell were you doing?"

"Wetting my fingers so I could turn the page."

What does an Australian girl use for protection during sex?
A bus shelter.

A woman from New York meets a tall Texan at a party. She asks in a very suggestive voice, "Is there anything I can do for you, handsome?"

"Well," replies the Texan, "I sure could use a piece of ass."

The woman from New York nods, takes the Texan into the bedroom, takes off all of her clothes, takes off all of his clothes, and engages in a hot session of mad passionate lovemaking with him. After they are done, she again says suggestively, "Now, handsome, is there anything else I can do for you?"

"Well, ma'am," he replies, "I could still use that piece of ass for my drink."

Have you ever wondered what a woman with PMS and a camel have in common?

They both retain water and fight like hell.

The judge called the lady up to the bench and asked if she could prove that the accused man was in the KKK.

She said, "I didn't say he was in the KKK. I said that he was a wizard under the sheets!"

What is the Australian men's foreplay?
"Are you awake?"

Three old ladies were sitting on a park bench having a quiet conversation when a flasher approached from across the park. The flasher came up to the ladies, stood right in front of them and opened his trench coat.

Marion immediately had a stroke.

Then Helen also had a stroke.

But Eleanor, being more feeble, couldn't reach that far.

What's the difference between a boyfriend and a husband?
Forty five minutes.

Have you ever noticed that as inflation goes up, so does the rate of interest? The same is true with women's skirts.

I have noticed a difference between the Jewish American Princess and the Mexican American Princess.

The Mexican American Princess has fake jewelry, but her orgasms are real.

The three words men hate to hear most during sex.
"Are you in?"

The three words women hate to hear most during sex.
"Honey, I'm home."

A chap staying at the Ritz Hotel in London removes a card offering sexual services from a telephone box on Piccadilly. Back at the hotel he rings the number.

A lady with a silky soft voice answers and asks if she can be of assistance.

The gentleman says, "I would like a blow job, missionary style, some doggie-style, some mild bondage, and finishing off with a boob wank."

The lady says, "It sounds intriguing sir, but you might first like to press nine to get an outside line."

What is it when a man talks nasty to a woman?
Sexual harassment.

What is it when a woman talks nasty to a man?
Four dollars a minute.

An elderly man and woman meet in a bar and get talking. They are enjoying their conversation so much that, when the bar closes, they decide to continue at the woman's apartment.

After a time, things start getting pretty romantic and they wind up in bed.

Afterward, they are both lying there, staring at the ceiling.

The old man is thinking, "If I had known she was a virgin, I would have been more careful with her."

The old lady is thinking, "If I had known he could get it up, I would have taken off my panties."

What do a coffin and a condom have in common?
They are both filled with stiffs, but one is coming, and one is going.

What is the similarity between oral sex and lobster thermidor?
You can't get either of them at home.

What makes men chase women they have no intention of marrying?
The same urge that makes dogs chase cars they have no intention of driving.

What's the difference between a terrorist and a woman with PMS?
You can negotiate with the terrorist.

According to archaeologists, for millions of years Neanderthal man was not fully erect.
That is easy to understand considering how ugly Neanderthal women were.

Why is it so hard for women to find men that are sensitive, caring, and good-looking?
Because those men already have boyfriends.

A woman walked into the pharmacy and asked for a vibrator. The pharmacist gestured with his index finger and said, "Come this way."

She said, "If I could come that way, I wouldn't need a vibrator."

A woman walks into a drugstore and asks the pharmacist if he sells extra large condoms.

He replies, "Yes we do. Would you like to buy some?"

She responds, "No sir, but do you mind if I wait around here until someone does?"

For months Bill had been Mary's devoted admirer.

At long last he had collected sufficient courage to ask her the momentous question.

Bill began, "There are quite a lot of advantages to being a bachelor, but there comes a time when one longs for the companionship of another being, a being who will regard one as perfect, as an idol. One whom one can treat as one's absolute own, who will be kind and faithful when times are hard and who will share ones joys and sorrows."

To his delight, Bill saw a sympathetic gleam in Mary's eyes. Then she nodded in agreement, "I think it is a wonderful idea. Can I help you pick the puppy?"

Why do driver's education classes in Redneck schools use the car only on Mondays, Wednesdays and Fridays?
Because on Tuesday and Thursday, the Sex Ed class uses it.

Medical science is so wonderful. Now after another million dollar study they have found out why women yawn and stretch in the morning.
It's because they have no balls to scratch.

So Jack was about to marry Liz who had been married many times before. He looked at her and said, "I know why I am here, but what I don't know is, how I can make it interesting."

Prospective husband: Do you have a book called 'Man, The Master of Women'?
Salesgirl: The fiction department is on the other side, sir.

McCormack walked into the bedroom and found his wife in bed with another man. "What's going on here? Who is this man?"

His wife replied, "That's a fair question." She turned to her lover and asked, "What's your name again?"

Mac went to the doctor to get a physical. A few days later the doctor saw Mac walking down the street with a gorgeous young woman on his arm. The doctor walked up to him and said, "You are really doing great, aren't you?"

Mac replied, "Just doing what you said, Doc. Get a hot mamma and be cheerful." The doctor replied, "I didn't say that. I said, 'You have got a heart murmur. Be careful'."

A rich man spotted a beautiful young lady sitting alone at a singles bar. "Say, baby, how about you coming home with me and giving me some head?"

She barely looked up. "That'll be the day."

Undaunted, he tried again. "Well, then, what if we go to my place and screw like rabbits?"

This time she snickered. "That'll be the day!"

"Okay," he said, "How about if we take my limo to my private jet, fly to Tahiti, and spend a week at my private beach?"

She looked up, smiled, and said, *"This will* be the day!"

What's the difference between love, true love, and showing off? Spitting, swallowing, and gargling.

When a woman lowers her voice, she wants something. If she raises it, it's a sign that she didn't get it.

Wedding and Honeymoon

Wedding Cake

A doctor was addressing a large audience regarding the evils of bad food.

The material we put into our stomachs is enough to have killed most of us sitting here, years ago.

Red meat is awful for you. Soft drinks corrode your stomach lining. Chinese food is loaded with MSG. High fat diets can be disastrous, and none of us realizes the long-term harm caused by the germs in our drinking water.

There is one thing that is the most dangerous of all, and most of us have, or will, eat it.

Can anyone here tell me what food it is that causes the most grief and suffering for years after eating it?

After several seconds of quiet, a seventy-five year old man in the front row, raised his hand and said, "Wedding cake."

First Time

One day a young cowboy and cowgirl decide to get married. After the wedding they begin their honeymoon. While driving down the road, the new bride sees two cows having sex.

The new bride asks, "What are they doing honey?" The husband answers, "They are roping."

She replies, "Oh, I see."

After a few more hours of driving they pass two horses having sex.

Again the young bride asks, "What are they doing honey?" The husband answers, "They're roping."

She replies, "Oh, I understand."

Finally they arrive at their hotel. They wash up and start to get ready for bed. When they get in the bed, they start to explore each other's bodies.

The bride discovers her husband's penis.

"What is that?" She asks. "That's my rope," He answers.

She slides her hands down further and gasps his nuts. "What are those?" she asks. "They are my knots," He answers.

Finally the couple begins to make love. After several minutes the bride says, "Stop honey, wait a minute.

Her husband asks, "What's the matter honey am I hurting you?"

She replies, "No. Undo those knots. I need more rope.

Wedding Night

A Chinese couple gets married, and she is still a virgin. He is also not very experienced.

On the wedding night, she cowers naked under the bed sheets as her husband undresses.

He climbs in next to her and tries to be reassuring, "My darring" he says, "I know dis yo firs time and you berry frighten. I promise you, I give you anyting you want, I do anyting, jus anyting you want, you say now, whatchou want?"

A thoughtful silence follows and he waits patiently and eagerly for her request.

She eventually replies shyly and unsure, "Please husband, I want a numba sixty nine."

More thoughtful silence, this time from him. Eventually, in a puzzled tone he asks, "You want Beef wif Broccori?"

Motherly Advice

A young woman got married, and she was a virgin who knew nothing of the ways of love.

On her wedding night, she ran downstairs to her mother and cried, "Momma, momma, what do I do?"

Her mother replied, "Don't you worry. Just lie back and enjoy yourself."

So the girl went back upstairs to where her husband was waiting. When she entered the room, she found that he had removed his shirt, and his arms and chest were very broad, and very hairy.

She ran screaming back down the stairs. "Momma, momma," she cried. "He has a big hairy chest."

Her mother calmly replied, "Don't you worry. His big hairy chest, that just means he has a large love muscle. You go back up there and have a good time."

So back up the stairs she went. This time her husband had removed his trousers, and she saw his strong, muscled, hairy legs.

She ran screaming back down the stairs. "Momma," she cried. "He has thick hairy legs."

Her mother calmly replied, "Don't you worry. His thick hairy legs just mean he has a large pecker. You go back up there and lie down and enjoy yourself."

So back up she goes. As she enters the room, she sees his feet for the first time and one of them is half missing.

She ran screaming back down the stairs. "Momma," she cried. "He has a foot and a half."

Her mother pushed her and said, "Out of my way, girl. This is a job for your mother."

Newlyweds

A young couple, each a virgin, was to be married the next day. The groom, Chris, confessed to his father, "Pa, I am scared to death. I don't know anything about sex!"

"Don't worry, Chris," replied his dad. "Your mother and I may have been a little overly protective, but I promise to make it up to you. Tomorrow night, I'll hide outside your hotel room door. If you need any advice, just say the word and I will be there to help."

The wedding went off perfectly, the new bride and groom settled into the hotel for their wedding night, but Chris was still nervous so he undressed in the bathroom.

The bride waited and waited, but no groom. She needed to use the bathroom in the worst way, but was too embarrassed to knock.

When Ann could wait no more, she grabbed a shoe box from the closet, squatted over it, and deposited a considerable load. Relieved, she got in bed, turned off the lights, and waited for her new groom.

When Chris finally got up his courage and came out of the bathroom, he stepped in the shoe box. Feeling around at his feet, he cried out, "Oh, my goodness, this box is full of crap!"

A voice came in from the hallway, "Turn her over, boy!"

The Wedding Dress

Jennifer's wedding day was fast approaching. Nothing could dampen her excitement, not even her parent's nasty divorce.

Her mother found the perfect dress to wear and would be the best-dressed mother-of-the-bride ever.

A week later, Jennifer was horrified to learn that her father's new young wife had bought the exact same dress as her mother.

Jennifer asked her father's new young wife to exchange it, but she refused.

"Absolutely not. I look like a million bucks in this dress, and I'm wearing it," she replied.

Jennifer told her mother who graciously said, "Never mind sweetheart. I'll get another dress. After all, it's your special day."

A few days later, they went shopping and her mother found another gorgeous dress.

When they stopped for lunch, Jennifer asked her mother, "Aren't you going to return the other dress? You really don't have another occasion where you could wear it."

Her mother just smiled and replied, "Of course I do, dear. I will wear it to the rehearsal dinner the night before the wedding."

First Night

A guy out on the golf course takes a high speed ball right in the crotch. Writhing in agony, he falls to the ground.

When he finally gets himself to the doctor, he says," How bad is it doc? I'm going on my honeymoon next week and my fiancé is still a virgin."

The doctor said, "I'll have to put your penis in a splint to let it heal and keep it straight. It should be okay by next week."

He took four tongue depressors, formed a neat little four-sided bandage, and wired it all together.

The guy mentioned none of this to his girl.

They get married and on their wedding night in the motel room, she rips open her blouse to reveal a gorgeous set of breasts.

This was the first time he had seen them.

She says, "You will be the first, no one has ever touched these breasts."

He whips down his pants and says, "Look at this. Mine is still in the crate."

Size Counts

A man and woman have been dating for quite a while and their relationship turns serious. The man proposes and his girlfriend accepts.

The girl tells him that there is something he should know. "My boobs are very small. They are just babies."

The man says, "I love you and measurements don't matter to me."

Then he tells her, "I also have a confession to make my penis is like a baby as well."

She says, "I love you so much size doesn't matter."

Finally the wedding and all goes well. That night the happy couple checks into the honeymoon suite at the hotel.

The blushing bride was in the bathroom putting on a sexy outfit. Her husband is in bed waiting. As she enters the bedroom, she reminds him of her confession about her boobs being small.

"Don't worry honey," he says.

She takes off her nightgown and her boobs are the smallest he's ever seen.

"It's my turn to undress," says the husband, "Now remember my confession about my penis size."

As he take his pants off the new bride says, "My God, I thought you said your penis was like a baby's?"

"It is, six pounds and seventeen inches long," he says.

Honeymoon Night

A honeymoon couple is in the Watergate Hotel in Washington. The bride is concerned, and asks, "What if the place is still bugged?"

The groom says, "I'll look for a bug." He looks behind the drapes, behind the pictures, under the rug.

Finally, he says, "Aha!"

Under the rug was a disc with four screws. He gets his Swiss army knife, unscrews the screws, and throws them and the disc out the window.

The next morning, the hotel manager asks the newlyweds, "How was your room? How was the service? How was your stay at the Watergate Hotel?"

The groom says, "Why are you asking me all of these questions?"

The hotel manager says, "The couple in the room under yours complained that the chandelier fell on them."

****

Paddy was planning to marry and asked his doctor how he could determine if his new bride is still a virgin. His doctor said, "Aye, Paddy, you need an Irish Do-It-Yourself Virginity Test Kit."

"And what might that be?" asked Paddy.

The doctor responded, "Some red paint, blue paint, and a shovel."

"Aye, but what would I be doin' with those things, doc?"

The doctor replied, "Before ye climb into bed on your wedding night, you paint one of your balls red and the other one blue. If she says, 'That's the strangest pair of balls I ever did see,' you hit her with the shovel."

First Nightie

A young woman was preparing for her wedding. She asked her mother to buy a nice long black negligee and carefully place it in her suitcase so it would not wrinkle.

Mom forgot until the last minute.

She dashed out to the store and because of the short time she had, she could only find a short pink nightie. She bought it and threw it into the suitcase.

After the wedding, the bride and groom entered their hotel room.

The groom was a little self-conscious, so he asked his new bride to change in the bathroom and promise not to peek while he got ready for bed.

While she was in the bathroom, the bride opened her suitcase and saw the negligee her mother had thrown in there.

"Oh no, it's short, pink, and wrinkled." She exclaimed.

Her groom cried out, "I told you not to peek."

Three Honeymoons

A mother had three virgin daughters, who were all getting married within a short time period. She worried about how their sex life would get started, so she made them all promise to send a postcard from the honeymoon with a few words on how marital sex felt.

The first girl sent a card from Hawaii two days after the wedding. The card said nothing but Nescafe. Mom was puzzled at first, but then went to the kitchen and got out the Nescafe jar. It said, "Good till the last drop." Mom blushed, but was pleased for her daughter.

The second girl sent the card from Vermont a week after the wedding, and the card read Benson and Hedges. Mom now knew to go straight to her husband's cigarettes, and she read from the Benson and Hedges pack, "Extra long, king size." She was again slightly embarrassed, but happy for her daughter.

The third girl left for her honeymoon in the Caribbean. Mom waited for a week, nothing. Another week went by, and still nothing. Then, after a whole month, a card finally arrived.

Written on the card, in shaky handwriting, were the words, British Airways. Mom took out her magazines and flipped through the pages, fearing the worst. Finally she found an ad for the airline. The ad said, "Three times a day, seven days a week, both ways."

Mom fainted.

Honeymoon Laundry

A young couple got married. On their honeymoon they were very anxious to consummate the marriage, because they were both virgins. They had saved themselves for the right partner and for marriage.

Because of their sexual inexperience they were a bit uncomfortable discussing the subject so they came up with the term 'doing the laundry' to use in place of 'making love' or 'having sex'. This made them both more comfortable with the whole concept.

The first night of their honeymoon was wonderful. They both had many years of pent up sexual frustration to expend so they 'did the laundry' no less than five times that first night and finally fell asleep together, completely exhausted.

In the middle of the night the new husband woke up and he was ready to 'do the laundry' again. He gently shook his new wife and asked her, "Can we do the laundry again?"

She was very tired and all of this new activity had taken its toll on her body. She told him that she just couldn't do it again just yet, maybe in the morning.

A few hours later the new wife wakes up feeling very guilty. Her new husband had saved himself for her for many years. What he had asked for wasn't unreasonable and she decided she should go ahead and 'do the laundry' with him again.

She gently shook him and said "honey, I am sorry I denied you. We can 'do the laundry' again if you want."

He replied, "That's OK. It was a small load, so I did it by hand."

Newlyweds

A week after their marriage, the redneck newlyweds paid a visit to their doctor. The husband says, "You aren't going to believe this doc, my thingie is turning blue."

"That's pretty unusual. Let me examine you."

The doctor takes a look, and sure enough, his penis is blue.

The doctor turns to the wife and asks, "Are you using the diaphragm that I prescribed for you?"

"Yep, sure am," she replied.

"And what kind of jelly are you using with it?"

"Grape."

Quick Marriage

A man met a beautiful lady and he decided he wanted to marry her immediately.

She protested, "But we don't know anything about each other."

He replied, "We will learn about each other as we go along."

She consented, and they were married, and went on a honeymoon to a very nice resort.

One morning, they were lying by the pool when he got up off his towel, climbed up to the ten meter board and did two and a half tuck gainer, entering the water perfectly, almost without a ripple. This was followed by a three rotations in jackknife position before he again straightened out and cut the water like a knife. After a few more demonstrations, he came back and lay down on his towel.

She said, "That was incredible!"

He said, "I used to be an Olympic diving champion. You see, I told you we would learn more about ourselves as we went along."

Now it was her turn, so she got up, jumped in the pool, and started doing laps. She was moving so fast that the froth from her pushing off at one end of the pool would hardly be gone before she was already touching the other end of the pool.

She did laps in freestyle, breast stroke, and butterfly.

After about thirty laps, completed in mere minutes, she climbed back out and lay down on her towel, barely breathing hard.

"That was incredible! Were you an Olympic endurance swimmer?"

"No," she said, "I was a hooker in Detroit and I worked both sides of the river."

New Husband

In a small town in the Old Country, the rabbi died. His widow was so troubled that the people of the town decided that she ought to get married again. However, the town was so small that the only eligible bachelor remaining was the town butcher.

The poor widow was somewhat dismayed because she had been wed to a scholar and the butcher had no great formal education, but she was lonely and agreed to marry him.

After the marriage, Friday came. She went to the Jewish ritual bath to get rid of impurities. Then, she went home to light the candles.

The butcher leaned over to her and said, "My mother told me that after the mikvah and before lighting the candles, it's a mitzvah to have sex." So they did.

She lit the candles. He leaned over again and said, "My father told me that after lighting the candles it's good to have sex." So they did.

They went to bed after prayers. When they awoke he said to her, "My grandmother said that before you go to the synagogue it's a mitzvah to have sex." So they did.

After praying all morning, they came home to rest. He whispers in her ear, "My grandfather says after praying it's a mitzvah to have sex." So they did.

On Sunday she went out to shop for food and met a friend who asked, "So how is the new husband?"

She replied, "Well, he is no scholar, but he comes from a wonderful family."

Two Weeks After

A young couple had been married for two weeks. The husband, although very much in love, couldn't wait to go party with his old drinking buddies.

He said to his new wife, "Honey, I'm going out, I'll be right back."

She asked, "OK coochey coo. Where are you going?"

"I'm going to the bar, pretty face."

She said, "Do you want a beer, my love?" She opened the refrigerator and displayed thirty five types of beer from all over the world.

He didn't know how to react, but said, "Yes, honey pie, but at the bar they have frozen glasses."

She replied, "Do you want a frozen glass poopsie?" She took a huge frozen mug from the freezer and offered it to him.

He was a bit pale, but managed to say, "Yes sweetums, but at the bar they have hors d'oeuvres that are really delicious. I'll be back soon."

You want hors d'oeuvres pookie? She opened the oven and took out ten different dishes of chicken wings, pigs in blankets, sausages, mushroom caps, pork strips, and things he had never seen.

"But baby, at the bar, there is the camaraderie, swearing, and dirty words from my friends that I miss."

"You want dirty words my precious. Well, listen up stink wad, drink your damned beer in your damned frozen mug and eat your flipping snacks, because you are not going anywhere. Do you understand, bunghole?"

And they lived happily ever after.

Honeymoon is Over

Moving in

Before: She wears teddies and suspenders, and you hold your farts in until she leaves the room. She's a gorgeous sex kitten and you tell her so. You are so sweet and adorable, and blowjobs follow ambient dinners like a fine port.

After: She farts in her grungy flannel bottoms while hypnotized by TV. You scratch your nuts unashamedly and bitch about work. Oral sex is over, and the new girl in the office really does have a great butt.

Addictions

Before: You tell her you don't mind an occasional cold beer on a hot day with your mates, and that you have taken recreational drugs, but those days are well and truly over.

After: For the fifth night in a row you stagger in blotto, dig out your stash and mull up, pass out in the lounge in your underpants, and expect her to accept that you are just being you.

Bodily Functions

Before: You spray aerosol after a crap, piss on the side of the bowl to reduce noise and never, ever fart in her presence.

After: You fart in front of her with impunity and obvious pride, commenting on the food intake for the day and speculating on the resultant odor. Despite repeated pleas to the contrary, you fart in bed and hold her head under the covers. You think it's hilarious.

Relations and Friends

Before: Her aunty Jane is a real character with a lively personality and interesting views about politics, and her unemployed girlfriend Laurie is a genuine, charming supportive friend who you think is very nice.

92

After: Aunty Jane is a loud-mouthed, pain-in-the-ass fascist with all the personality of a cold sore. Laurie is a manipulative loser, but you wouldn't mind doing her if the opportunity arose.

Sex

Before: Sex is a sweat-soaked, gymnastic romp that lasts for hours. You screw to impress, using all your tricks, like your renowned boob grope, marathon oral sex sessions, and jackhammer-like screwing. Screwing four times a day is not uncommon.

After: A wank is often preferable to the effort of sex. When you do have sex, you think about Shirley.

Attention Span

Before: Her words are hypnotic, her wit is incisive, and her anecdotes about her life pre-you are spellbinding. Over candlelight and coffee you listen with interest and politely chortle as she recounts stories of her childhood.

After: Your eyes glaze over as soon as she mentions anything that doesn't involve you. What's more, you develop the uncanny ability to be able to concentrate on the TV and listen to her at the same time. The phrase, "Are you listening to me?" becomes an evening mantra.

Overall Evaluation

Before: She thinks you are witty, disciplined, a sexual athlete, attentive, loving, faithful, and devoid of all crass male habits which have plagued her previous relationships, but she does suspect that you might be full of shit.

After: She knows you are full of crap.

Wedding Story

A man longs to wed a maiden with her virtue intact. He searches for one, but resigns himself to the fact that every female over the age of sixteen in his town has already been at it.

Finally, he decides to take matters in hand and adopts a baby girl from the orphanage. He raises her until she is walking and talking and then sends her away to a monastery for safekeeping until marrying age.

After many years she finally reaches maturity and he retrieves her from the monastery and marries her. After the wedding they make their way back to his house and into the bedroom where they both prepare themselves for the consummation.

They lie down together in his bed and he reaches over for a jar of petroleum jelly.

"Why the jelly," she asks him?

"So I do not hurt your most delicate parts during the act of lovemaking," he replies.

"Why don't you just spit on your pecker like the monks did?"

Marriage Quickies

A man has a voice in everything his wife buys – an invoice.

A marriage license, like a fishing license, doesn't guarantee a prize catch.

When a man marries a woman, they become one; but the trouble starts when they try to decide which one.

Psychiatrists tell us women tend to marry men like their fathers. Now we know why mothers cry at weddings.

An old man goes to the Wizard to ask him if he can remove a curse he has been living with for the last forty years.

The Wizard says, "Maybe, but you will have to tell me the exact words that were used to put the curse on you."

The old man says, "I now pronounce you man and wife."

Some women study law in school and become lawyers.
Other women become wives and lay down the law.

Loving is easy. It's the living together that is so damned hard.

A couple was having a discussion about family finances. Finally the husband exploded, "If it weren't for my money, the house wouldn't be here!" The wife replied, "My dear, if it weren't for your money I wouldn't be here."

A wife is a person who finishes her husband's sentences for him, then tells him why he is wrong.

Trouble in marriage often starts when a man gets so busy earning his salt, that he forgets his sugar.

Too many couples marry for better, or for worse, but not for good.

No love is more inspiring than that of the long-married couple, where he still considers a joy to behold and she still considers it a joy to be held.

Many girls like to marry a military man - he can cook, sew, and make beds, is in good health, and he is already used to taking orders.

How do most men define marriage? A very expensive way to get your laundry done free.

A newly married man was discussing his honeymoon. He says to his buddy at lunch, "Last night, I rolled over, tapped my beautiful young wife on the shoulder, gave her a wink, and we had ourselves a performance. Later that night, about two am, I rolled over, gave my sweetie a nudge, and we had ourselves another performance. Being so newly married and not yet tired of the task, I waited quietly in bed while my beauty slept until I couldn't wait any longer. It was four am when I gave her a little nudge. She opened her blue eyes and smiled sweetly. We immediately had ourselves a rehearsal."

"A rehearsal?" his buddy asks, "Don't you mean a performance?"

"No, because a rehearsal is when nobody comes."

When I got married I told my wife I wanted to set the world on fire. After three years of being married, I wanted to set myself on fire.

On anniversaries, the wise husband always forgets the past, but never the present.

A foolish husband says to his wife, "Honey, you stick to the washing, ironing, cooking, and scrubbing. No wife of mine is going to work."

A man goes to the doctor and is told he has only six hours to live. He rushes home and tells his wife and then says lets make love. They do and then fall asleep.

A couple of hours later he wakes up and says, "Honey, let's do it again." They do and again, after a very brief nap he says to her, "Honey, how about doing it one more time?"

She replies, "No. I have to get up in the morning, you don't."

Many a man falls in love with a dimple and makes the mistake of marrying the whole girl.

The wedding guest was remarking to the bride, "You look absolutely darling." Then she whispered, "What happened to that blonde with the frizzy hair that your husband used to date?"

The bride answers, "I died my hair!"

A doctor examined a woman, took the husband aside, and said, "I don't like the looks of your wife."

The man replied, "I don't either, doc, but she is a great cook and really good with the kids."

Japanese scientists have created a camera with a shutter speed so fast, they can now photograph a woman with her mouth shut.

A man goes to a shrink and says, "Doctor, my wife is unfaithful to me. Every evening, she goes to Larry's bar and picks up men. In fact, she goes to bed with anybody who asks her. I am going crazy. What do you think I should do?"

"Relax," says the doctor, "Take a deep breath and calm down. Now, tell me, where exactly is Larry's bar?"

Man: "My sister just married an Irishman!"
Friend: "Oh, really?"
Man: "No, O'Reilly."

Mrs. Jones was reading a letter at breakfast. Suddenly she looked up suspiciously at her husband.

"Henry," she said, "I just received a letter from mother saying she isn't accepting our invitation to come and stay, as we do not appear to want her. What does she mean by that? I told you to write and say that she was to come at her own convenience. You did write, didn't you?"

"Yes I did, but I couldn't spell 'convenience', so I wrote 'risk'."

Wife gets naked and asks hubby, "What turns you on more, my pretty face or my sexy body?"

Hubby looks her up and down and replies, "Your sense of humor."

My wife got me to believe in religion.
Really?
Yeah, until I married her I didn't believe in hell.

A married man was visiting his girlfriend when she requested that he shave his beard. "Oh James, I like your beard, but I would really love to see your handsome face."

James replied, "My wife loves this beard, I couldn't possibly do it, she would kill me."

"Oh please?" the girlfriend asked again, in a sexy little voice.

"Really, I can't," he replies. "My wife loves this beard."

The girlfriend asked once more, and he sighs and finally gives in. That night James crawls into bed with his wife while she was sleeping.

The wife is awakened somewhat, feels his face and replies, "Oh Michael, you shouldn't be here, my husband will be home soon."

My wife is a sex object - every time I ask for sex, she objects.

A wife shows her husband a silk handkerchief and asks him, "Doesn't this belong to your secretary?"
" Where did you find that?" he stutters.
"I didn't," she answers. "The mailman found it in your night-stand."

If a man has enough horse sense to treat his wife like a thoroughbred, she will never turn into an old nag.

The bonds of matrimony are a good investment, only when the interest is kept up.

A husband shouts down to his wife, "Come upstairs and look at this magnificent clock.
She rushes upstairs only to find her husband standing in the bedroom completely naked.
"That's not a clock," she exclaims.
"It soon will be when it has two hands and a face on it," he replies.

Bubba and Earl are fishing and sipping soda pop when Bubba suddenly says, "I am thinking of divorcing my wife. She hasn't spoken to me in six months."

Earl looks at his friend, takes a swig of his soda and, after a moment says, "You better think it over. Women like that are hard to find."

Two guys, one old and one young, are pushing their carts around Home Depot when they collide. The old guy says to the young guy, "Sorry about that. I'm looking for my wife, and I guess I wasn't paying attention to where I was going."

The young guy says, "That's OK. It's a coincidence. I am looking for my wife, too. I can't find her and I am getting a little desperate."

The old guy says, "Maybe we can help each other. What does your wife look like?

The young guy says, "She is twenty-five years old, tall with red hair, blue eyes, long legs, big boobs, and she is wearing tight white shorts.

What does your wife look like?"

The old guy says, "Doesn't matter. Let's look for yours."

How can you tell if your wife is dead?
The sex is the same, but the dishes pile up.

How can you tell if your husband is dead?
The sex is the same, but you get the remote.

A married slut goes on holiday without her husband to Bermuda. On her first night, she meets a tall young guy in a bar. It's not long before they are back at her room and they do the deed. As he is leaving she asks his name. He replies, "Snow." She laughs, he looks puzzled. She then explains, "My husband is never going to believe I had ten inches of snow in the Caribbean."

Bigamy is when you have one wife too many; monogamy is the same.

Marriage is the chief cause of divorce.

GUTS - is arriving home late after a night out with the guys, being assaulted by your wife with a broom, and having the guts to ask, "Are you still cleaning, or are you flying somewhere?"

BALLS - is coming home late after a night out with the guys, smelling of perfume and beer, lipstick on your collar, slapping your wife on the butt and having the balls to say, "You're next."

Lena folded and put away Ole's underwear. Ole took out a pair the next morning and noticed there was powder all over the crotch area. He started to shake the powder out and said, "Darn it, Lena, I vish you vouldn't put so much talcum powder in my undervear."

Lena replied, "Dat's not talcum powder, Ole. Dat's Miracle Gro."

A good Catholic gentleman went to confession and told the priest that he got drunk and had sex with a woman six times.

The priest asked who the harlot was.

The man replied that it was his wife.

The priest explained that sex was supposed to be a part of marriage and why would the man feel compelled to confess.

The man said there was no one else who would believe him.

What's the difference between secretaries and wives?
Secretaries get a little behind at work. Wives get a big behind at home.

A truly happy marriage is one in which the woman gives the best years of her life to the man who makes them the best years.

An old couple was sitting on the porch rocking when suddenly the old woman knocked the old guy out of his chair and on to the ground.

He got up, dusted himself off and asked her, "Why did you hit me?"

She told him, "It is because your pecker is too small."

He sat back down for a while, then he knocks her out of her chair.

She asked him, "Why did you hit me?"

"Because after fifty years you have something to compare it to."

As long as your wife tries to improve your table manners, your grammar, your posture, your attire and station in life, you know at least, that she still loves you.

Marrying an old bachelor is like buying second hand furniture.

Did you hear about the guy from Alabama who passed away and left his entire estate to his beloved widow? She can't touch it until she is fourteen.

On his honeymoon, an elderly man turned to his young bride, complaining, "Darling, you are going to kill me. How can I tell if I am having an orgasm or a heart attack?"

"That's easy," she responded. "If you grab your chest, it is a heart attack. If you grab mine, it's an orgasm."

Marriage is a lot like living in an earthquake zone. You never know when some little fault will shake the whole house.

An Air Force sergeant and a general were sitting in the barbershop. They were both just getting finished with their shaves, when the barbers reached for some after-shave to slap on their faces.

The general shouted, "Hey, don't put that stuff on me. My wife will think I have been in a whorehouse."

The sergeant turned to his barber and said, "Go ahead and put it on me. My wife doesn't know what the inside of a whorehouse smells like."

A man comes home early from work one day and sees his wife, on all fours scrubbing the floor, wearing nothing but a silk bathrobe. He sneaks up behind her, lifts up her robe, has his way with her and then smacks her in the head.

She turns around and says, "After you do something so nice, why would you hit me in the head like that?"

He snaps back, "That's for not looking to see who it was."

Every husband and wife knows that when one loses their temper the other catches it.

The cowboy and his wife were in town to get supplies while a mountain lion broke into their cabin and ate all of their food, knocked over the furniture, and ate his most prized possession, a brand new pair of five hundred dollar boots.

When the couple returned and saw the mess and the left over toe of one of the boots, the cowboy said that he would get that cat if it was the last thing he did.

He immediately loaded his rifle and went out hunting.

He was gone for three days when he finally bagged his prey. He skinned it and returned home. Upon arrival, he threw it triumphantly on the floor in front of his wife.

She looked up and said, "Hey, is that the cat that chewed your new shoes?"

What is it called when a woman is paralyzed from the waist down? Marriage.

How are a Texas tornado and a Tennessee divorce the same? Somebody is going to lose a trailer.

One Saturday afternoon, a man was sitting in his lawn chair, drinking beer, and watching his wife mow the lawn.

The neighbor lady from across the street was so outraged that she came over and shouted, "You should be hung."

He took a drink from his beer, wiped the cold foam from his lips, lifted his darkened sunglasses, stared directly at the woman and replied, "I am, that's why she cuts the grass."

I haven't spoken to my wife in eighteen months - I don't like to interrupt her.

A man comes home to find his wife packing her bags. "Where are you going?" he asked.

"To Las Vegas, I found out that there are men that will pay me four hundred dollars to do what I do for you for free."

The man thought for a moment, and began packing his bags.

"What do you think you are doing?" she asked.

"I'm going to Las Vegas with you. I want to see how you live on eight hundred dollars a year."

A preacher was telling his congregation that anything they could think of, old or new, was discussed somewhere in the Bible and that the entirety of the human experience could be found there.

After the service, he was approached by a woman who said, "Preacher, I don't believe the Bible mentions PMS."

The preacher replied that he was sure it must be in there somewhere and that he would look for it.

The following week after service, the preacher called the woman aside and showed her a passage which read, "And Mary rode Joseph's ass all the way to Bethlehem."

The woman applying for a job in a Florida lemon grove seemed way too qualified for the job. The foreman asked, "Do you have any actual experience in picking lemons?"

"As a matter if fact, yes." she replied. "I have been divorced three times."

A woman, her husband, and their four rambunctious young sons were in their car waiting at a traffic light. The woman glanced over at the car next them, noticing a blissfully happy mother with her baby daughter.

Looking at her husband she said, "As soon as I lose my weight from the last baby, I want to try for a daughter."

The husband reached up to the dash, grabbed an open box of snacks, and said, "Here, have another cookie."

John and Tom were discussing popular family trends on sex, marriage, and values.

John said, "I didn't sleep with my wife before we got married, did you?"

Tom replied, "I'm not sure, what was her maiden name?"

A man came home from work, sat down in his favorite chair, turned on the TV, and said to his wife, "Quick, bring me a beer before it starts."

She looked a little puzzled, but brought him a beer. When he finished it, he said, "Quick, bring me another beer. It's gonna start."

This time she looked a bit angry, but brought him a beer. When it was gone he said, "Quick, another beer before it starts."

"That's it!" She blows her top. "You bastard! You waltz in here, flop your fat ass down, don't even say hello to me, and then expect me to run around like your slave. Don't you realize that I cook, and clean, and wash, and iron all day long?"

The husband sighed, "Damn, it started.

Love is grand - divorce is several hundred grand.

Late on Sunday night, after a weekend of TV sports a wife is getting ready for bed and says to her husband, "It's twenty to twelve."

He looks over toward her and asks, "Who's winning?"

A husband and wife were enjoying some horizontal recreation. The husband stopped and asked his wife, "Did I hurt you?"

She replied. "No, why?"

He responded, "You moved."

A new law recently passed in South Carolina
Even after a couple gets divorced, they are still brother and sister.

Mac walked into a bar and ordered martini after martini, each time removing the olives and placing them in a jar.

When the jar was filled with olives and all the drinks consumed, Mac started to leave.

The man sitting next to him asked, "Excuse me sir. What was that all about?"

Mac replied, "My wife just sent me out for a jar of olives."

My wife has a slight impediment in her speech -
every now and then she stops to breathe. - *Jimmy Durante*

Some people think that wife should be spelled WIIFF meaning, "What's in it for females."

A lady walks into the drug store and asks the druggist for some arsenic.

The druggist asks, "What do you want with arsenic?"

The lady says, "To kill my husband."

"I can't sell you any for that reason," says he druggist.

The lady reaches into her purse and pulls out a photo of a man and a woman in a compromising position, the man is her husband and the lady is the druggist's wife.

He looks at the photo and says, "Oh, I didn't know you had a prescription."

A good wife always forgives her husband when she is wrong. (Milton Berle)

During a recent vacation in Las Vegas, a man went to see a popular magic show. After one especially amazing feat, a man from the back of the theater yelled, "How did you do that?"

"I could tell you, sir," the magician answered, "But then I would have to kill you."

After a pause, the man yelled back, "OK, then just tell my wife."

A couple was driving down a country road for several miles, not saying a word. An earlier discussion had led to an argument and neither of them wanted to concede their position.

As they passed a barnyard of mules, goats, and pigs, the wife asks sarcastically, "Relatives of yours?"

"Yep," the husband replies, "In-laws."

Last week I went to the doctor and he gave me a pain reliever, but it didn't work. When I got home, my wife was still there.

Two men were talking. "So, how's your sex life?" asks the first man.

"Oh, nothing special," replies the second. "I'm having Social Security sex."

"Social Security sex? What the heck is that?" asks the first man.

"You know. I get a little each month, but not enough to live on."

Wife: You don't deserve a wife like me.
Husband: I also have arthritis, and I don't deserve that either.

A guy goes on vacation to the Holy Land with his wife and mother-in-law. The mother-in-law dies so they go to an undertaker. He explains that he can ship the body home, but that it'll cost over five thousand dollars, whereas they can bury her in the Holy Land for only a hundred fifty dollars.

The guy says, "We will ship her home."

The undertaker asks, "Are you sure? That's an awfully big expense and we can do a very nice burial here."

The guy says, "Over two thousand years ago they buried a guy here and three days later he rose from the dead. I just don't want to take that chance."

"Cash, check, or charge?" the clerk asked, after folding items the woman wished to purchase.

As she fumbled for her wallet the clerk noticed a remote control for a television set in her purse.

"Do you always carry your TV remote?" he asked.

She said, "No, but my husband refused to come shopping with me, so I figured this was the most evil thing I could do to him."

A man is in his back yard trying to fly a kite. He keeps throwing it into the air, where the wind catches it for a few seconds, before it comes crashing back down.

Watching him from the kitchen window, his wife mutters how men have to be told how to do everything. She opens the window and yells, "You need more tail."

He shouts back, "Make up your mind. Last night you told me to go fly a kite."

Do you know why women fake orgasm?
Because men fake foreplay.

A husband was in big trouble when he forgot his wife's birthday. His wife told him, "Tomorrow there better be something in the driveway for me that goes from zero to two hundred in under ten seconds."

The next morning the wife found a small package in the driveway. She opened it and found a brand new bathroom scale.

Funeral arrangements for the husband have been set for Saturday.

A man was in an accident and his penis was chopped off. He was rushed to the hospital, where the doctor examined him. After careful examination the doctor said, "We can replace it with a small size for $2,000, a medium size for $5,000, or an extra-large size for $10,000. I realize it's a lot of money, so take your time and talk it over with your wife."

When the doctor came back into the room, he found the man staring sadly at the floor. "We have decided," the man told him as he choked back tears. "My wife says she would rather have a new kitchen."

All eyes were on the radiant bride as her father escorted her down the aisle. They reached the altar and the waiting groom then the bride kissed her father and placed something in his hand.

The guests in the front pews responded with ripples of laughter. Even the preacher smiled broadly as her father gave her away in marriage, the bride gave him back his credit card.

After a quarrel, a wife said to her husband, "You know, I was a fool when I married you." The husband replied, "Yes, dear, but I was in love and didn't notice."

A lady walked into a pharmacy and spoke to the pharmacist.

She asked, "Do you have Viagra?"

"Yes," he answered.

She asked, "Does it work?"

"Yes."

"Can you get it over the counter?"

"I can if I take two," he answered proudly.

Joe was driving home from one of his business trips in Northern Arizona when he saw an elderly Navajo walking on the side of the road.

As the trip was a long and quiet one, he stopped the car and asked the Navajo man if he would like a ride. After a bit of small talk, the Navajo man noticed a brown bag on the seat next to Joe.

The Indian asked, "What's in the bag?"

Joe looked down at the brown bag and said, "It's a bottle of wine. I got it for my wife."

The Navajo was silent for a moment then speaking with the quiet wisdom of an elder said, "Good trade."

A wife was making a breakfast of fried eggs for her husband. Suddenly her husband burst into the kitchen.

"Careful. Careful. Put in some more butter. Oh my God. You're cooking too many at once. Too many. Turn them. Turn them now. We need more butter. Oh my God. Where are we going to get more butter? They are going to stick. Careful. Careful. I said, be careful.

You never listen to me when you are cooking. Never. Turn them. Hurry up. Are you crazy? Have you lost your mind? Don't forget to salt them. You know you always forget to salt them. Use the salt. Use the salt, use the salt."

The wife stared at him. "What the hell is wrong with you? Do you think I don't know how to fry a couple of eggs?"

The husband calmly replied, "I wanted to show you what it feels like when I am driving with you in the damn car."

Marriage is the triumph of imagination over intelligence. Second marriage is the triumph of hope over experience.

Two old folks got married. As they were lying in bed in their wedding suite, staring at the ceiling, the old man says, "I haven't been completely honest with you. I think the world of you, but you are only number two to me. Golf is my first love. It is my hobby, my passion, my first love."

They both stare at the ceiling for a bit, then the woman says, "While we are baring our souls, I guess I better tell you that I have been a hooker all my life."

The man looks at her for a moment, then says, "Have you tried widening your stance and adjusting your grip?"

A man said to his wife, "Guess what I heard in the pub? They say the milkman has made love to every woman on our street except one."

She said, "I'll bet it's that stuck-up Mary at number twenty- three."

A seventy five year old wealthy widower named Chuck, shows up at the Country Club with a beautiful and very sexy twenty-five-year-old blonde with a gorgeous body.

His buddies at the club are all amazed. They corner him and ask, "Chuck, how did you get the trophy girlfriend?"

Chuck replies, "Girlfriend? She's my wife!"

"So, how did you persuade her to marry you?"

He says, "I lied about my age."

His friends respond, "What do you mean? Did you tell her you were only fifty?"

He smiles and says, "No, I told her I was ninety nine."

Why is divorce so expensive?
It's worth it.

While assisting in an exam on a young woman who came to the ER with lower abdominal pains, the doctor asked her if she were sexually active. The young woman appeared slightly embarrassed by the question, but replied, "No, I just lay there."

What's the difference between a new husband and a new dog?

After a year, the dog is still excited to see you.

I have a friend whose wife tried to cut him off. . .
But she couldn't find out where he was getting it.

There are two guys, one rich and the other poor, talking about what they bought their wives for Christmas.

The rich guy says I bought my wife a diamond ring and a Mercedes Benz.

The poor guy says why the ring and the car.

He says well if she doesn't like the ring she can take it back in her Mercedes Benz.

The poor guy says he bought his wife a pair of slippers and a dildo.

The rich one says why the slippers and the dildo.

He says if she doesn't like the slippers she can go screw herself.

A couple is lying in bed one night when the husband turns to his wife and begins to kiss her and stroke her skin. "Oh honey, I can't tonight," the wife apologizes, "I have a gynecologist appointment tomorrow."

The man turns over, sulks for awhile, then asks, "Honey, you don't happen to have a dentist appointment tomorrow, do you?"

A computer company distributed a corporate-clothing catalogue that included a pair of cuff links. One was inscribed Ctrl (Control) and the other Esc (Escape), just as they look on a computer keyboard.

The woman said, "They would make a good present for any man, If only to remind him of the two things he can never have."

He used to love her until she became his awful wedded wife.

A woman worries about the future until she gets a husband.
A man never worries about the future until he gets a wife.
A successful man is one who makes more money than his wife can spend.
A successful woman is one who can find such a man.

Do you know the difference between fear and panic?

Fear is when you realize for the first time that you can't do it the second time.

Panic is when you realize for the second time that you can't do it the first time.

117

Two guys are talking over a beer, discussing various sexual positions. The first guy says his favorite position is the rodeo.

The other guy asks what the position is, and how to do it?

The first guy says, "You tell your wife to get on the bed on all fours and then do it doggy style.

Once things start to get underway and she is really enjoying it, lean forward and whisper in her ear, 'Your sister likes this position too' and then try to hang on for eight seconds."

The local IRS agent was investigating a claim by a single mother who said that she had ten boys all by the name of Oscar. He tried to catch her in the lie so he went to visit her at her home. When he arrived he asked her to bring the boys in.

She yelled out, "Oscar!" They all came in the house.

He was amazed and said, "How do you call them when you only want one?" She replied, "Oh, that's easy, I calls 'em by they last name."

During a wedding, the bride's mother managed to keep from crying until she glanced at her own parents.

Her mother had reached over to her father's wheelchair and gently touched his hand. That was all it took to start her tears flowing.

After the wedding, she went over to her old mother and told her how that tender gesture triggered her outburst.

"I am sorry to ruin your moment," her mother replied, "But I was just checking to see if he was still alive."

An escaped convict broke into a house and tied up a young couple who had been sleeping in the bedroom.

As soon as he had a chance, the husband turned to his voluptuous young wife, bound up on the bed in a skimpy nightgown, and whispered, "Honey, this guy hasn't seen a woman in many years. Just cooperate with him and do anything he wants. If he wants to have sex with you, just go along with it and pretend you like it. Our lives depend on it."

"Dear," the wife hissed, spitting out her gag, "I am so relieved you feel that way, because he just whispered to me he thinks you are really cute."

The man noticed a very beautiful woman in a large supermarket. He went up to her and said, "I've lost my wife here in the supermarket. Can you talk to me for a couple of minutes?"

The woman looked puzzled. "Why talk to me?" she asked.

"Because every time I talk to a woman with boobs like yours, my wife appears out of nowhere."

A mortician was working late one night. He examined the body of Mister Shubnell, about to be cremated, and made a startling discovery. Shubnell had the largest private part he had ever seen.

"I am so sorry Mister Shubnell," the mortician commented, "I can not allow you to be cremated with such an impressive private part. It must be saved for posterity."

So, he removed it, stuffed it into his briefcase, and took it home. "I have something to show you that you won't believe," he said to his wife as he opened his briefcase.

"My God." the wife exclaimed, "Shubnell is dead?"

Two men had not seen one another for some time and met at a bar. After inquiring about each other's health one asked how the other's wife was doing.

"She died last week. We went out to the garden to dig up a cabbage for dinner and she had a heart attack and dropped down dead, right there in the middle of the garden."

"I am very sorry," replied his friend. "What did you do?"

"I had a pizza delivered."

A golfer stands over his tee shot for what seems an eternity to his partner. He looks up, looks down, measures the distance, and figures the wind direction and speed. His partner continues to fidget.

Finally his exasperated partner says, "What's taking so long? Hit the blasted ball."

The guy answers, "My wife is up there watching me from the clubhouse. I want to make this a perfect shot."

"Forget it, man. You will never hit her from here."

In a small town, there is a factory that only recruits married men. One of the local women, LuAnn, was angry about this and demanded to speak to the manager to find out why.

Luann demanded to know, "Why is it you limit your employees to married men? Is it because you think women are weak, dumb, and cantankerous?"

"Not at all madam," the manager replied. "It is because male employees are used to obeying orders, accustomed to being shoved around, know how to keep their mouths shut, and don't pout when I yell at them."

An old woman, who was particularly despondent over the recent death of her husband, decided that she would kill herself and join him in death.

Thinking that it would be best to get it over with quickly, she took out his old Army pistol and made the decision to shoot herself in the heart since it was so badly broken in the first place.

Not wanting to miss the vital organ and become a vegetable and burden to someone, she called her doctor's office to inquire as to just exactly where the heart would be.

The doctor said, "Your heart would be just below your left breast."

Later that night, she was admitted to the hospital with a gunshot wound to her left knee.

One morning while making breakfast, a man walked up to his wife and pinched her on her butt and said, "You know if you firmed this up we could get rid of your girdle."

While this was on the edge of intolerable, she thought herself better and replied with silence. The next morning the man woke his wife with a pinch on the breast and said, "You know if you firmed these up we could get rid of your bra."

This was beyond a silence response, so she rolled over and grabbed him by his thingie. With a death grip in place she said, "You know if you firmed this up we could get rid of the postman, the gardener, the pool man, and your brother."

There are three stages of marital sex:
Honeymoon sex - You have sex three or four times a night.
Vacation sex - You have sex ten or twelve times a year.
Oral sex - You stand on the opposite side of the room from your spouse and yell, "Screw you."

121

A guy gets into his grubbiest clothes on a Saturday morning and sets about all the chores his wife has been hassling him to do for weeks. He cleans the garage, prunes the hedges, and is halfway through mowing the lawn when a very attractive woman pulls up in her car. She yells out of her window, "Say, what do you get for yard work?"

The guy thinks for a minute and answers,

"Sometimes the lady that lives here lets me sleep with her."

The ideal wife should be beautiful, but not so beautiful that people think you married her only for her beauty.

The ideal wife should be wealthy, but not so wealthy that people think you married her only for her money.

The ideal wife should be gentle, but not so gentle that she can't suck a tennis ball through a fifty-foot garden hose.

A couple had been married for thirty-five years and was celebrating their sixtieth birthdays, which fell on the same day. During the celebration a fairy appeared and said that because they had been such a loving couple for all thirty-five years, she would give them one wish each.

The husband wanted to travel around the world. The fairy waved her hand. Poof! He had the tickets in his hand.

Next, it was the wife's turn. She paused for a moment, and then said shyly, "I would like to have a man thirty years younger than me."

The fairy picked up her wand. Poof! She was ninety.

Did you hear about the Chinese couple that had a retarded baby? They named it Sum Ting Wong.

One neighbor said to another, "Mike, you should close the drapes on your bedroom window. I saw you making love to your wife last week."

Mike responded, "The joke is on you. I was gone on business all last week."

Why do couples hold hands during their wedding?

It's a formality, just like two boxers shaking hands before the fight begins.

When people discuss 'love marriage' vs. 'arranged marriage', it's like asking someone, if suicide is better than being murdered.

Before marriage, a man will lie awake all night thinking about something you said. After marriage, he will fall asleep before you finish.

With her marriage she got a new name and a dress.

"Honey," said this husband to his wife, "I invited a friend home for supper."

"What? Are you crazy? The house is a mess, I haven't been shopping, all the dishes are dirty, and I don't feel like cooking a fancy meal!"

"I know all that."

"Then why did you invite a friend for supper?"

"Because the poor fool is thinking about getting married."

❧ ❧

Do think marriage is a lottery?

No. With a lottery you have a slight chance.

❧ ❧

The best way to get most husbands to do something is to suggest that perhaps they are too old to do it. (Ann Bancroft)

❧ ❧

I think men who have a pierced ear are better prepared for marriage. They have experienced pain and bought jewelry. (Rita Rudner)

❧ ❧

Attending a wedding for the first time, a little girl whispered to her mother, "Why is the bride dressed in white?"

"Because white is the color of happiness, and today is the happiest day of her life."

The child thought about this for a moment, then said, "So why is the groom wearing black?"

❧ ❧

If women are such good multi-taskers, why can't they have a headache and sex at the same time?

❧ ❧

Keep your eyes wide open before marriage, half shut afterwards. (Benjamin Franklin)

❧ ❧

My wife dresses to kill. She cooks the same way. (Henny Youngman)

My wife and I were happy for twenty years. Then we met. (Rodney Dangerfield)

The secret of a happy marriage remains a secret. (Henny Youngman)

A man is suffering from extreme headaches so he goes to see his doctor.

"Doctor I seem to be having these bad headaches and nothing I do seems to cure them."

The doctor says, "One thing I always do to relieve my headaches is put my head between my wife's boobs and have her jiggle them until my headache goes away."

"Thanks doc, I think I'll try it."

Two weeks pass and the man goes back to his doctor.

The doctor says, "Well, have your headaches cleared up?"

"They sure have. I tried what you said. By the way I love the wall paper in your home."

A man asked an American Indian what his wife's name is.

The Indian replied, "She called Five Horses."

The man said, "That's an unusual name for your wife. What does it mean?"

The old Indian answered, "It old Indian name. It mean, NAG, NAG, NAG, NAG, NAG."

The Lord of the manor returned from his grouse hunt quite a bit earlier than expected. He entered the master bedroom to change, and found her Ladyship making passionate love to Sir John of Chapman.

The irate Lord stood stiffly and loudly berated his wife for her infidelity. With thunder in his voice, he reminded her that he had taken her from a miserable existence on a local run-down farm, given her a fine home, provided her with servants, expensive clothes, jewels, and almost anything else she desired.

By this time the woman was crying inconsolably, his Lordship then turned his wrath on his supposed friend, "And as for you Sir John, you might at least stop while I am talking!"

A husband said to his wife, "No, I don't hate your relatives. In fact, I like your mother-in-law better than I like mine."

Settling In

After Marriage

Before Marriage

127

Women and Wives

- Women are unpredictable. Before marriage, she expects a man, after marriage she suspects him, and after death she respects him.

- There was a guy who told his woman that he loved her so much that he would go thru hell for her. They got married - and now he is going thru hell.

- A man inserted an 'ad' in the classifieds: "Wife wanted." Next day, he received a hundred letters. They all said the same thing, "You can have mine."

- When a man opens the door of his car for his wife, you can be sure of one thing: either the car is new or the wife is.

- It's easy to tell if a man is married or not. Just watch him drive a car with a woman sitting beside him. If both his hands are on the wheel, he is married.

- A man received a letter from some kidnappers. The letter said, "If you don't promise to send us $100,000, we promise you we will kidnap your wife." The poor man wrote back, "I am afraid I can't keep my promise, but I hope you will keep yours."

- "What's the matter, you look depressed." "I'm having trouble with my wife." "What happened?" "She said she wasn't going to speak to me for thirty days." "But that ought to make you happy." "It did, but today is the last day."

Orgasm Lessons

A Jewish gentleman married a much younger woman. No matter what he did sexually, the wife never achieved orgasm.

Since a Jewish wife is entitled to sexual pleasure, they decide to ask the rabbi.

The rabbi listens to their story, strokes his beard, and suggests that they, "Hire a strapping young man and while the two of you are making love, have the young man wave a towel over you. That will help your wife fantasize and should bring on an orgasm."

They go home and follow the rabbi's advice. They hire a handsome young man and he waves a towel over them as they make love. It doesn't help and she is still unsatisfied, so they go back to the rabbi.

The rabbi says to the husband, "Try it reversed. Have the young man make love to your wife and you wave the towel over them."

Once again, they follow the rabbi's advice.

The young man gets into bed with the wife, while the husband waves the towel. The young man gets to work with great enthusiasm and the wife soon has an enormous, room-shaking, earsplitting, screaming orgasm.

The husband smiles, looks at the young man and says to him triumphantly, "You see, you young schmuck? That is how you should wave a towel."

First Surprise

Once upon a time, there lived a man who had an all-consuming passion for beans. He loved them with all of his heart. The one problem he had was the resulting flatulation and malodorous reaction.

One day he met a girl and fell in love. When the thought of marriage occurred to him, he thought to himself, "She is such a sweet girl; she may never go for my carrying on with my love affair with beans." He decided between the two and the girl won. He decided to give up beans for marriage.

Some months later he had car problems. On the way walking home he decided to call his new bride and share his tale of woe to explain why he would be late.

Along the way he passed a small deli and the smell of freshly baked beans overcame him. He thought that he had far enough to go so that any ill effects would be gone before he reached home, and he went in.

After consuming four large orders of the wonderful beans, he putt-putted his way down the road. By the time he reached home, he felt that all the remnants of the feast were gone.

His wife greeted him at the door and said that she had a surprise for him for dinner. She then proceeded to blindfold him and lead him to his favorite chair at the head of the table.

He sat down but before she could remove the blindfold, the phone rang. She made him promise not to remove the blindfold until she returned.

He used the opportunity to good purpose and shifted his weight to one side and let one rip. It was short but sweet and quite odiferous. With that he felt for the napkin and vigorously fanned the air about him.

Just as he began to regain his composure, he felt another attack coming and again shifting his weight, he let loose with another few bursts. These were real winners and he tried his best to clear the air about him.

While he tried to keep his ear on the phone conversation he managed to continue for at least five more minutes until his wife finished talking and hung up. He contentedly fiddled with his plate as best he could while being blindfolded.

She returned and apologized for taking so long and asked if he had peeked. He replied no and she removed the blindfold and he saw his surprise. . . eight dinner guests seated around the table.

Difficulties

A young farmer is newly married. He and his new bride can't get enough sex.

Just before leaving the house for the fields at dawn, they make love, and when he returns home in the evening they do it again before and after supper. Sometimes a few more times during the night.

The problem is that during the day, the fields are so far from the house that the young man loses a lot of time traveling home and back to the field at noon, so, he decides to ask his neighbor what to do.

"Easiest thing in the world," says the neighbor. "You take your rifle out with you every day don't you? Well, when you feel like you are in the mood for love, just fire a shot into the air. Your wife can use that as a signal to come to meet you in the field. That way you won't lose any working time."

He tries this and it seems to work pretty well for a while. One day the neighbor stops by the house to pay a visit and notices the young man sitting alone inside looking very sad.

"What's wrong?" he asks. "Didn't my idea work? And where's your wife?"

"Oh, it worked. Whenever I got in the mood I would fire off a shot like you said, and Sandy would come running. Then we would find a secluded place and do it for a while. When we finished Sandy would go back home."

"So what's the problem?"

"I think I overdid it. I haven't seen her since the hunting season started."

Comparison

A bum, who obviously has seen more than his share of hard times, approaches a well-dressed gentleman on the street. "Hey buddy, can you spare two dollars?"

The well-dressed gentleman responds, "You are not going to spend it on liquor are you?"

"No, sir, I don't drink," says the bum.

"You are not going to throw it away in some crap game, are you?" asks the gentleman.

"No way, I don't gamble," answers the bum.

"You wouldn't waste the money at a golf course for greens fees, would you?" asks the man.

"Never," says the bum. "I don't play golf."

The man asks the bum if he would like to come home with him for a home cooked meal and the bum accepts the invitation.

While they are heading for the man's house, the bum's curiosity gets the better of him. "Isn't your wife going to be angry when she sees a guy like me at your table?"

"Probably," says the man, "But it will be worth it. I want her to see what happens to a guy who doesn't drink, gamble, or play golf."

House Repairs

"Pa, you need to go out and fix the outhouse."

Pa replies, "There ain't nuthin wrong with the outhouse."

Ma yells back, "Yes there is; now git out there and fix it."

Pa mosies out to the outhouse, looks around and yells back, "Ma, there ain't nuthin wrong with the outhouse."

Ma replies, "Stick yur head in the hole."

Pa yells back, "I ain't stickin my head in that hole."

Ma says, "Ya have to stick yur head in the hole to see what to fix."

Pa sticks his head in the hole, looks around and yells back, "Ma, there ain't nuthin wrong with this outhouse."

Ma hollers back, "Now take your head out of the hole,"

Pa proceeds to pull his head out of the hole, then starts yelling, "Ma, help! My beard is stuck in the cracks in the toilet seat."

To which Ma replies, "Hurt's, don't it."

Work or Play

A man wonders if having sex on the Sabbath is a sin, because he is not sure if sex is work or play. He goes to a priest and asks for his opinion on this question.

The priest says, "My son, after an exhaustive search, I am positive that sex is work and is therefore not permitted on Sundays."

The man thinks the priest could be wrong and goes to a minister, who is a married man, and experienced in this matter.

The minister gave him the same reply as the priest, "My son, sex is work and therefore not for the Sabbath."

Not pleased with the reply, he seeks out the ultimate authority, a man who possesses thousands of year's tradition and knowledge. He consults a rabbi.

The rabbi immediately replies without hesitation, "Sex is definitely play."

The man asks, "Rabbi, how can you be so sure when so many others tell me sex is work?"

The Rabbi speaks wisely, "If sex were work, my wife would have the maid do it."

Lost Wife

One day, while a woodcutter was cutting a branch of a tree above a river, his ax fell into the river. When he cried out, the Lord appeared and asked, "Why are you crying?"

The woodcutter said that his ax had fallen into water, and he needed it to make his living.

The Lord went down into the water and reappeared with a golden ax. "Is this your ax?" The Lord asked.

The woodcutter replied, "No."

The Lord again went down and came up with a silver ax. "Is this your ax?" the Lord asked.

Again, the woodcutter replied, "No."

The Lord went down again and came up with an old iron ax. "Is this your ax?" the Lord asked.

The woodcutter replied, "Yes."

The Lord was pleased with the man's honesty and gave him all three axes to keep, and the woodcutter went home happy.

Some time later the woodcutter was walking with his wife along the river bank, and his wife fell into the river. When he cried out, the Lord again appeared and asked him, "Why are you crying?"

"Oh Lord, my wife has fallen into the water."

The Lord went down into the water and came up with Angelina Jolie. "Is this your wife?" the Lord asked.

"Yes," cried the woodcutter.

The Lord was furious. "You lied. That is an untruth."

The woodcutter replied, "Oh, forgive me, my Lord. It is a misunderstanding. You see, if I had said 'no' to Angelina Jolie, you would have come up with Heather Locklear. Then if I also said 'no' to her, you would have come up with my wife. Had I then said 'yes' to her, you would have given me all three.

Lord, I am a poor man, and am not able to take care of all three wives, so that's why I said yes to the first one."

The moral of this story is: Whenever a man lies, it is for a good and honorable reason, and for the benefit of others.

Sarcasm

An attorney got home late one evening after a very taxing day trying to get a stay of execution for a client, James Wright, who was due to be hanged for murder at midnight.

His last-minute plea for clemency to the governor had failed and he was feeling worn out and depressed.

As soon as the lawyer got through the door at home, his wife started on him with, "What time of night do you call this? Where have you been?"

Too shattered to play his usual role in this familiar ritual, he poured himself a glass of whisky and headed off for a long hot soak in the bathtub, pursued by the predictable sarcastic remarks.

While he was in the bath, the phone rang. The wife answered and was told that her husband's client had been granted his stay of execution after all.

Finally realizing what a day he must have had, she decided to go upstairs to give him the good news.

As she opened the bathroom door, she was greeted by the sight of her husband's rear end as he was bent over naked drying his legs and feet.

"They are not hanging Wright tonight," she said.

He whirled around and screamed, "For crying out loud woman, don't you ever stop!"

Doubting Her Fidelity

Mac, a salesman, is scheduled to travel cross country for a meeting with one of his suppliers, which meant his wife would be alone for a week.

This worried Mac, since he had caught Laura eyeing men on and off for the last few months. He decided to go down to the mall, to a little sex shop, where he could buy her a play toy, in hopes of diverting her sexual energy.

The next day he went there on his lunch break and is met by a little Chinese man. "Hewwo, how may I hep you?"

"I'm going out of town next week, and I don't trust my wife by herself. What can you give me to occupy her while I am gone, so she doesn't find another man?"

The little man thinks for a second and says, "I have perfect cure for woman who be horny." He goes back through a beaded curtain, and returns a minute later with a dusty, gray box. "This exacry what you need."

The little man opens the box and moves over a bit into the light. Mac peers inside, and sees what looks like an ordinary dildo.

"What's so special about that? I can get that anywhere," he says.

The little man smiles and says, "No sir, this Voodoo pecker."

"Voodoo pecker. What the heck is Voodoo pecker?" says Mac.

"You watch crosry," replies the little man, and then says, "Voodoo pecker, the door."

To Mac's amazement, the dildo slowly levitates out of the box, and heads for the door. When it gets to the door, it lunges back and forth and back and forth at it, reducing it to splinters until nothing is left of it. It then returns to the box and floats gently inside.

After witnessing this, he says, "I must have it. It's perfect. How much is it?"

"Two tousan dorrar," says the little man.

"Two thousand dollars, that's highway robbery." says Mac.

"OK, misser, if you no want it."

"I'll take it," concedes Mac.

Mac gets home, and his wife meets him at the door. "What's in the box?" she asks. "Oh nothing," says Mac.

"Please tell me. Please, please!"

"OK, it's for you, a special present," Mac says, and opens the box. Laura glances inside and sees the dildo. "What is it?"

"It's a Voodoo pecker. When I'm gone, and you get real horny, just open this box, and say, 'Voodoo pecker my crotch.' and you will be completely satisfied," he says.

"What will happen?" she asks.

"You'll see, just wait"

Two days later, Mac's on his trip. His wife is getting horny and thinks, "Gee, I think it's time to try out this Voodoo pecker thingy."

She gets the box, opens it up, and peers inside. She sets the box down, and gets undressed and sits back on the bed. She reaches part way into the box, and thinks for a moment, and draws her hand back out. "Voodoo pecker, my crotch," she says.

It floats out of the box, and heads right for her crotch. It gets to her, and enters her, lunging back and forth. She lays back on the bed, thinking that this is the most incredible thing she has ever felt. She has one orgasm, two, three, and it's still going. How does she get it to stop? Four. . . five. Oh my, I have to get this thing to stop.

I'll have to drive to the hospital for help. They will surely know how to stop it.

She puts a dress on, gets the keys to her car, and heads out; all the while Voodoo pecker is still going at her. She is in the car driving down the road, having her sixth and seventh orgasms.

She is having difficulty concentrating on driving. She looks in her mirror and sees flashing red and blue. "Oh, damn a cop."

She pulls over.

The cop walks up to the car, "Good evening, may I see your license, proof of insurance, and registration please?"

"S-s-sure officer. It's r-r-r-right h-h-here," She hands it to him.

"Have you been drinking tonight lady?"

"N-n-n-no I haven't o-o-o-officer. I have to get t-t-to the h-h-hospital."

"Are you sick? What's the problem?" the cop says.

"I have a Voodoo pecker in my crotch and it won't come out."

"A what?" the cop asks.

"A Voodoo p-p-pecker-r-r. P-p-p-please. . ."

The cop thinks about it for a second. Then looks at her, and says, "Voodoo pecker, my ass!"

Paddys Wife

Paddy O'Reilly hoisted his beer and said, "Here's to spending the rest of me life, between the legs of me wife!"

That won him top prize for the best toast of the night at the small town pub.

He went home and told his wife, Mary. "I won the prize tonight for the best toast of the night."

She said, "Aye, what was your toast?"

Paddy said, "Here is to spending me life, sitting in church beside me wife."

"Oh, that is very nice indeed, Paddy." Mary said.

The next day, Mary ran into one of Paddy's toasting buddies on the street corner.

The man chuckled leeringly and said, "The other night Paddy won the prize with a toast about you, Mary."

She said, "Aye, and I was a bit surprised me self. You know, he has only been there twice. Once he fell asleep and the other time I had to pull him by the ears to make him come."

Lost Interest

Doc, you have to help me. My wife just isn't interested in sex anymore. Don't you have a pill or something I can give her?"

"I can't prescribe. . ."

"Doc, we have been friends for years. Have you ever seen me this upset? I am desperate. I can't think, I can't concentrate, and my life is going utterly to hell. You must to help me."

The doctor gets a small bottle of pills. "Ordinarily, I wouldn't do this. These are experimental pills. The tests so far indicate that they are very powerful. Don't give her more than one, just one."

"I don't know doc, she's awfully cold."

"One. No more. Put it in her coffee."

"OK."

The guy expresses gratitude and leaves for home, where his wife has dinner waiting. When dinner is finished, she goes to the kitchen to bring dessert.

The man hastily pulls the pills from his pocket and drops one into his wife's coffee. He reflects for a moment, hesitates, and then drops in a second pill.

Then he begins to worry, so he drops one pill into his own coffee.

His wife returns and they enjoy their dessert and coffee. A few minutes after they finish, his wife shudders a little, sighs deeply, and a strange look comes over her. In a near-whisper and a tone of voice he has never heard her use before, she says, "I need a man."

His eyes glitter and his hands tremble as he replies, "Me too."

Best Husband

A group of men are sitting in a sauna discussing business and stocks when suddenly a cell phone rings. One of them picks it up.

"Hi honey, are you at the club?"

"Yes, dear."

"Honey you won't believe this, but I'm standing in front of Herme's and there is a beautiful mink on sale in the window."

"How much is it, dear?"

"They are giving it away for only five thousand dollars. Can you believe it?"

"But you already have fur coats."

"Please dear it's absolutely exquisite."

"Fine, go ahead and buy it."

"Thank you sweetheart. Oh, not to keep you much longer, I passed by the Mercedes dealership this morning and saw their new convertible. It was to die for! I talked to the salesman and the one in the showroom is brand new, leather seats, power everything. What do you think??"

"Honey, come on, we already have cars."

"You promised me that I could get a convertible."

"How much is it?"

"You won't believe it, but he said he would let us have it for ninety-five grand, fully loaded with all the options."

"OK, OK dear, go ahead and purchase it."

144

"I love you. You are the best husband a wife could ask for. I hope I'm not pushing it, but remember our trip we took to Paris? Remember the Brown's place with the swimming pool and tennis courts?

It's on the market to be sold. I saw it this morning at the Real Estate agency. If we bought it we would have a perfect place to stay during the cold winter months."

"I had actually thought about it. You say it's on the market?"

"Really, you were actually thinking about it? Can I go make an offer on it? You know it's not listed very high, and it would be perfect for our type of lifestyle."

"How much is it listed at?"

"Only eight-twenty-five, sweetheart. It's a steal."

"I guess we have the money. Go ahead and make an offer, but no more than eight twenty."

"This is turning out to be a great day. Can't wait to see you later tonight to celebrate."

"See you tonight dear."

The man shuts off the cell phone and asks, "So, who does this phone belong to?"

Caught in the Act

A farmer was sitting in the neighborhood bar getting drunk. A man came in and asked the farmer why he was sitting there on such a beautiful day getting drunk?

The farmer said, "Some things you just can't explain."

The man asked, "What happened that is so horrible?"

The farmer said, "Well, if you must know, today I was sitting by my cow milking her. Just as I got the bucket about full, she took her left leg and kicked it over."

The man said, "That's not so bad, what's the big deal?"

The farmer said, "Some things you just can't explain. I took her left leg and tied it to the post on the left with some rope. Then I sat down and continued to milk her. Just as I got the bucket about full again she took her right leg and kicked it over."

The man asked, "Again?'

The farmer said, "Something's you just can't explain. I took her right leg and tied it to the post on the right."

The man asked, "So then what did you do?"

The farmer said, "I sat back down and continued to milk her, and just as I got the bucket just about full, the stupid cow knocks over the bucket with her tail."

The man asked, "Wow, you must have been pretty upset."

Then the farmer said, "Some things you just can't explain. I didn't have any more rope, so I took off my belt and tied her tail to the rafter. In that moment, my pants fell down and my wife walked in."

His and Her Stories

Her story -

My husband was in an odd mood Saturday night. We planned to meet at a café for a drink. I spent the afternoon shopping with the girls and I thought it might have been my fault because I was a bit later than I promised, but he didn't say anything much about it.

I don't remember doing anything to make him upset, but could tell there was something wrong. The conversation was quite slow going so I thought we should go off to some place intimate so we could talk more privately.

We went to this restaurant and he was still acting a bit funny. I was getting very worried, what did I do? What was bothering him? Was he mad at me? I tried to cheer him up, but kept wondering what was bothering him. Was it me or something else?

I asked him if he was upset with me, and he said no, but I wasn't really sure. So anyway, in the car on the way back home, I said that I loved him deeply and he just put his arm around me. I didn't know what the heck that meant, because you know, he didn't say it back or anything.

We finally got back home and I was wondering if he was going to leave me. I tried to get him to talk, but he just switched on the TV. Reluctantly, I said I was going to go to bed.

Then after about ten minutes, he joined me and to my surprise, we made love. He still seemed really distracted, so afterwards I just wanted to confront him but I just cried myself to sleep. I just don't know what to do anymore. I think he is seeing someone else.

His story -

Played badly today. Shot 87. Can't putt for shit. Felt kind of tired. Got laid though.

Great Performance

After a few years of married life, an engineer finds he is unable to perform. He goes to his doctor, and his doctor tries a few things but nothing works. Finally the doctor says to him, "This is all in your mind," and refers him to a psychiatrist.

After a few visits, the shrink confesses, "I am at a loss as to how you could possibly be cured." Finally the psychiatrist refers him to a witch doctor.

The witch doctor says, "I can cure this." He throws powder on a flame and there is a flash with billowing blue smoke.

The witch doctor says, "This is a powerful healing, but you can only use it sparingly. All you have to do is say "123" and it will rise as long as you wish."

The guy is curious and then asks the witch doctor, "What happens when it's over?"

The witch doctor says, "All you or your partner has to say is '1234' and it will go down. Be warned though, it will not work again for six more months."

The guy goes home and that night he is ready to surprise his wife with the good news. He is lying in bed with her and says, "123," and suddenly he gets a huge erection.

His wife turns over and says, "What did you say, '123' for?"

Mother-In-Law

A married couple was in a terrible accident in which the woman's face was severely burned.

The doctor told the husband that they could not graft any skin from her body because she was too thin, so the husband offered to donate some of his own skin. However, the only skin on his body that the doctor felt was suitable would have to come from his buttocks.

The husband and wife agreed that they would tell no one about where the skin came from, and requested that the doctor also honor their secret.

After the surgery was completed, everyone was astounded at the woman's new beauty. She looked more beautiful than she ever had before. All her friends and relatives commented about her new youthful beauty.

One day, she was alone with her husband, and she was overcome with emotion at his sacrifice. She said, "Dear, I want to thank you for everything you did for me. There is no way I could ever repay you."

"My darling," he replied, "Think nothing of it. I get all the thanks I need every time I see your mother kiss you on the cheek."

Headaches

It was a warm, sunny Sunday, so a man and his wife decided to go to the zoo. They spent the day, and at closing time they walked past the gorilla cage, and the man noticed the gorilla was intently looking at his wife.

"That gorilla is getting excited just looking at your boobs," he said.

"Why don't you take your blouse off and we will see what he does?"

At first she declined, but was finally persuaded by her husband. She took off her blouse and bra and faced the gorilla.

The gorilla went nuts. He started grunting and jumping up and down in his cage.

"Hey," the husband said, "Let's see what would happen if you take off all your clothes and dance in front of him."

Again she said no, but once again he persuaded her.

This time the ape really went crazy He climbed up and down the bars, did flips, ran around in circles, and tossed his food all over the cage.

The husband went over to the cage, opened the door, and pushed his wife in. "Now," said the husband, "Tell <u>him</u> you have a headache."

How Many Partners

A man took his wife to the County Fair and they walked around one of the exhibits of breeding bulls.

They went up to the first pen and there was a sign that said, "This white-ribbon bull mated fifty times last year."

The wife poked her husband in the ribs and said, "He mated fifty times last year."

They walked a little further and saw another pen with a sign that said, "This prize bull mated one hundred twenty times last year."

The wife hit her husband on the shoulder and said, "That's more than twice a week. You could learn a lot from him."

As they walked further, they saw a third bull pen with a sign saying, "This winning bull mated three hundred and sixty five times last year."

The wife was really excited and said, "That's once a day. You could really learn something from this one."

The husband looked at her and said, "Go up and ask the owner if it was with the same cow."

151

What Women Want

Young King Arthur was ambushed and imprisoned by the monarch of a neighboring kingdom. The monarch could have killed him, but was moved by Arthur's youth and ideals. The monarch offered him freedom, as long as he could answer a very difficult question. Arthur would have a year to figure out the answer. If, after a year, he still had no answer, he would be put to death.

The question: What do women really want?

Such a question would perplex even the most knowledgeable man and, to young Arthur, it seemed an impossible query. However, since it was better than death, he accepted the monarch's proposition to have an answer by year's end.

He returned to his kingdom and began to poll everybody, including the princess, the prostitutes, the priests, the wise men, and the court jester. He spoke with everyone, but no one could give him a satisfactory answer.

Many people advised him to consult the old witch. They said that only she would know the answer. The price would be high as the witch was famous throughout the kingdom for the exorbitant prices she charged.

The last day of the year arrived and Arthur had no alternative but to talk to the witch. She agreed to answer his question, but he would have to accept her price first. The old witch wanted to marry Sir Gawain, the most noble of the Knights of the Round Table and Arthur's closest friend.

Young Arthur was horrified. She was hunchbacked and hideous, had only one tooth, smelled like sewage, and made obscene noises. He had never encountered such a repugnant creature. He refused to force his friend to marry her and have to endure such a burden.

Sir Gawain, upon learning of the proposal, spoke with Arthur. He told him that nothing was too big a sacrifice compared to Arthur's life and the preservation of the Round Table.

Hence, their wedding was proclaimed, and the witch answered Arthur's question by telling him, "What a woman really wants is to be in charge of her own life."

Everyone instantly knew that the witch had uttered a great truth and that Arthur's life would be spared. And so it was. The neighboring monarch granted Arthur total freedom.

What a wedding Gawain and the witch had. Arthur was torn between relief and anguish. Gawain was proper as always, gentle and courteous. The old witch put her worst manners on display, and generally made everyone very uncomfortable.

The honeymoon hour approached. Gawain, steeling himself for a horrific experience, entered the bedroom, but what a sight awaited him. The most beautiful woman he had ever seen lay before him. The astounded Gawain asked what had happened.

The beauty replied that since he had been so kind to her when she had appeared as a witch, she would henceforth be her horrible, deformed self half the time, and the other half she would be her beautiful maiden self. She asked him, which would he want her to be during the day, and which during the night?

What a cruel question. Gawain pondered his predicament. During the day, a beautiful woman to show off to his friends, but at night, in the privacy of his home, an old witch, or would he prefer having by day a hideous witch, but by night a beautiful woman with whom to enjoy many intimate moments?

Noble Gawain replied that he would let her choose for herself. Upon hearing this, she announced that she would be beautiful all the time, because he had respected her enough to let her be in charge of her own life.

Moral of the story: If a woman doesn't get her own way, things are going to get ugly.

Cold Shoulder

A couple had been married fifteen years. One afternoon they were working in the garden together.

As the wife was bending over pulling weeds, the husband said, "Hey honey you are getting fat. Your butt is getting huge. I bet it is as big as the gas grill."

The husband felt he needed to prove his point, so he took a yardstick, measured the grill, and then measured his wife's butt.

"Yep, he said, "Just what I thought, just about the same size.

The wife became very incensed and decided to let him finish the gardening alone. She went inside and didn't speak to her husband for the rest of the day.

That evening when they went to bed, the husband cuddled up to his wife and said, "How about a little lovemaking?"

The wife turned her back to him, and gave him the cold shoulder.

"What's the matter?" he asked.

She replied, "You don't think I am going to fire up this big ass grill for one little weenie, do you?"

Cookbook Diary

Monday: It's fun to cook for Tom. Today I made angel food cake. The recipe said separate and beat twelve eggs. The neighbor was nice enough to loan me some extra bowls.

Tuesday: Tom wanted fruit salad for supper. The recipe said serve without dressing. So I didn't wear any clothes. What a surprise when Tom brought a friend home for supper.

Wednesday: A good day for rice. The recipe said wash thoroughly before steaming the rice. It seemed kind of silly, but I took a bath anyway then dried my beautiful blonde hair. I can't say it improved the rice any.

Thursday: Today Tom asked for salad again I tried a new recipe. It said to prepare ingredients, lay on a bed of lettuce one hour before serving. Tom asked me why I was rolling around in the garden.

Friday: I found an easy recipe for cookies. It said put the ingredients in a bowl and beat it. There must have been something wrong with this recipe. When I got back, everything was the same as when I left.

Saturday: Tom did the shopping today and brought home a turkey. He asked me to dress it for Sunday. I don't have any clothes that fit it, and for some reason Tom keeps counting to ten.

Sunday: Tom's folks came to dinner. I wanted to serve roast, but all I had was hamburger. Suddenly I had a flash of genius. I put the hamburger in the oven and set the control for roast. It still came out hamburger, much to my disappointment.

This has been a very exciting week. I am eager for tomorrow to come so I can try out a new recipe for Tom. If I can talk him into buying a bigger oven, I would like to surprise him with a chocolate moose.

Bad Comparison

A man staggers into an emergency room with two black eyes and a golf club wrapped tightly around his throat.

Naturally, the doctor asks him what happened.

"I was having a quiet round of golf with my wife when she sliced her ball into a pasture of cows."

"We went to look for it and while I was rooting around, I noticed one of the cows had something white at its rear end."

"I walked over and lifted up the tail and sure enough, there was my wife's golf ball. It was stuck right in the middle of the cow's butt. That's when I made my mistake."

"What did you do?" asks the doctor.

I lifted the tail and yelled back to my wife, "Hey, this one looks like yours."

Garden Chores

A man is doing yard work and his wife is about to take a shower.

The man realizes that he can't find the rake. He yells up to his wife, to look out the window and says, "Where is the rake?"

She can't hear him and shouts back, "What?"

The man first points to his eye, then points to his knee and finally makes a raking motion.

The wife is not sure and says, "What?"

The man repeats his gestures. He points to his eye, then points to his knee, and finally makes a raking motion (eye - knee - the rake.)

The wife understands and signals back. She first points to her eye, next she points to her left breast, then she points to her butt, and finally to her crotch.

There is no way in heck the man can even come close to understanding that one.

Exasperated, he goes upstairs and asks her, "What in the heck was that you were trying to tell me?"

She replies, "eye - left tit - behind - the bush."

Viagra

A woman asked her husband if he would like some breakfast. "Would you like bacon and eggs, perhaps? A slice of toast and maybe some grapefruit and coffee?" she asked.

He declined and told her, "It's this Viagra," he said. "It has really taken the edge off my appetite."

At lunchtime, she asked if he would like something else, like a bowl of homemade soup, homemade muffins, or a cheese sandwich.

He declined again and said, "The Viagra, really trashes my desire for food."

About dinnertime, she asked if he wanted anything to eat. Would he like maybe a steak and apple pie? Maybe he would like a pizza or a tasty stir-fry?

He declined again and said, "No thanks, I am still not hungry."

She finally said, "Well then, would you mind letting me get up? I'm starving."

♪ ♪ ♪

A man falls asleep on the beach under the mid-day sun and suffers severe sunburn to his legs. He is taken to hospital and by the time he gets there his skin has turned bright red. Anything that touches his legs causes him tremendous pain.

The doctor takes a long look at him and then prescribes intravenous feeding of water and electrolytes, a mild sedative, and Viagra.

The nurse is astounded and asks, "What good will Viagra do him in that condition?"

"Simple," replies the doctor, "It will keep the sheet off his legs."

Hold Me

One evening last week, my wife and I were getting into bed. The passion started to heat up, and she eventually said, "I don't feel like it, I just want you to hold me."

I said, "What are you talking about?"

She uttered the words that every husband dreads. She explained that I was not in tune with her emotional needs as a woman.

I realized that nothing was going to happen, so I went to sleep.

The next day, we went shopping at a big department store. I walked around while she tried on three very expensive outfits. She couldn't decide which one to take, so I told her to take all three of them.

She then related that she wanted matching shoes worth two hundred dollars each. I agreed and said that it would be fine.

Then we went to the Jewelry Department where she picked up a set of diamond earrings. She was so excited. She must have thought that I was losing my mind, but I don't think she cared. I believe she was testing me when she asked for a tennis bracelet, because she doesn't even play tennis. I know it surprised her when I told her that it was also fine.

She was almost sexually excited from all of this and you should have seen the delight on her face when she said, "I am finished shopping, let's go to the cash register."

That's when I blurted out, "No, honey. I don't feel like buying all this stuff right now." Her face went completely blank.

I said, "I just want you to hold this stuff for a while." Just when she had this look like she was going to kill me, I added, "You must not be in tune with my financial needs as a man."

I think we might resume having sex again, sometime next year.

Ladies Night Out

A woman played cards with her bridge club every Thursday night. After a peaceful game or two with the ladies, she went home to fix supper for her husband and herself.

One Thursday, she is playing a great game. She has an incredible hand. Suddenly, she notices the time. "I have to get home to fix supper. My husband's going to be really angry if it's not on the table when he gets home." She dashes out of her friend's house without finishing the hand.

When she gets home, she realizes that all she has in the cupboard is a wilted lettuce leaf, an egg, and a can of cat food.

In a panic, she opens the can of cat food, stirs in the egg, and garnishes it with the lettuce leaf just as her husband is pulling into the driveway. She watches in horror as he sits down to eat, then realizes, he loves it.

"Mmm, darling, this is the best meal you have made in the forty years we have been married. You can make this for me any day. That night, they had sex for the first time in months.

Every Thursday from then on, she made the same dinner for her husband. She told her bridge cronies about it and they were all horrified. "You are going to kill him," they said. Disregarding their objections, she continued to make him his cat food dinner and then they would screw like rabbits.

Two months later, her husband died. The Thursday after the funeral, all the bridge women attacked the new widow for being so callous.

"You killed him. We told you that feeding him that cat food every week would do him in. How can you just sit there so calmly and play bridge, knowing you murdered your husband?"

The widow replied, "I did not kill him. He fell off the window sill while he was licking his ass."

Ten Times More

A man was out golfing one day and one of them hit his ball into the woods. He went into the woods to look for it and found a frog stuck in a trap. The frog said to him "If you release me from this trap, I will grant you three wishes."

The man freed the frog and the frog said, "Thank you, but I failed to mention that there was a condition to your wishes. Whatever you wish for, your wife will get ten times more or better."

The man said, "That would be fine. His first wish was that he wanted to be the most handsome man in the world.

The frog warned him, "You do realize that this wish will also make your wife the most beautiful woman in the world, such a beauty, that men will flock to her."

The man replied, "That will be fine, because I will be the most handsome man and she will only have eyes for me."

POOF! He is the most beautiful man in the world.

For his second wish, he wanted to be the richest man in the world.

The frog said, "That will make your wife the richest woman in the world and she will be ten times richer than you."

The man said, "That will be fine, because what is mine is hers and what is hers is mine."

POOF! He is the richest man in the world.

The frog then asked about his third wish and he answered, "I would like a mild heart attack."

Princess

Once upon a time there lived a king. The king had a beautiful daughter.

Everything the girl touched would melt. No matter what, metal, wood, plastic, etc. Everything she touched would melt. Because of this, men were afraid of her and nobody would dare to marry her.

One day a wizard told the king, "If your daughter touches one thing that would not melt in her hands, her affliction will be cured." The king was overjoyed.

The next day, he held a competition. Any man that can bring his daughter an object that would not melt gets to marry her and inherit the king's wealth.

Three young princes took up the challenge. The first prince brought a huge diamond, thinking that diamond is the hardest object, and therefore will not melt. Alas, once the princess touched it, it melted. The prince went away.

The second prince brought a very hard alloy, but the same thing happened, so he too went away.

The third prince told the princess, "Put your hand in my pocket and feel it."

The princess did as told. Ta Da! It did not melt.

The king was overjoyed and the third prince lived happily with the princess ever after.

He knew - M & Ms melt in your mouth, not in your hand.

162

Anniversary Surprise

To celebrate fifty years of marriage, a couple booked a weekend at St. Andrews Golf Club.

On the third tee, the husband said, "Darling, I have to confess something. Twenty years ago I had a brief affair. It meant nothing. I hope that you can forgive me."

His wife was hurt but said, "Dearest, those days are long gone. What we have now is far more valuable. I forgive you."

They embraced and kissed.

On the seventeenth tee the wife said to her husband, "Darling, since we are being honest with each other, I have something to tell you. Fifty-two years ago I had a sex change operation. I was a man before we met."

The husband threw a fit. He cursed, threw his driver away, broke the rest of his clubs one by one, and tore at his clothes.

He screamed and ranted, "You liar. You despicable cheat. How could you? I trusted you, and you have been playing off from the ladies' tee all these years."

Sex Seasons

An elderly married couple scheduled their annual medical exams the same day so they could travel together.

After the husband's examination, the doctor said to him, "You appear to be in good health. Do you have any medical concerns that you would like to discuss with me?"

"In fact, I do," said the man. "After I have sex with my wife for the first time, I am usually hot and sweaty. And then, after I have sex with my wife the second time, I am usually cold and chilly."

"This is very interesting," replied the doctor. "Let me do some research and get back to you."

After examining the elderly wife, the doctor said to her, "Everything appears to be fine. Do you have any medical concerns that you would like to discuss with me?"

The lady replied that she had no questions or concerns.

The doctor then asked her, "Your husband had an unusual concern. He claims that he is usually hot and sweaty after having sex the first time with you and then cold and chilly after the second time. Do you know why?"

"That old buzzard." she replied. "That's because the first time is usually in July and the second time is in December."

Underwear Tease

A lady who had been married for several years was growing more and more frustrated at her husband's lack of interest in sex.

She wondered about ways to add some pizzazz to their sexual relationship, and finally decided to purchase some crotchless underwear she had seen in a lingerie shop.

One evening when she was feeling particularly desirous, and he was as usual, watching television, she took a shower, freshened up, and put on the crotchless undies and a slinky negligee.

She strolled between her husband and the television, and suggestively tossed one leg up on his chair arm.

"Want some of this?" she purred.

"Are you kidding? Look what it already did to your underwear."

Paying for It

It all began when the young bride approached her new husband on their wedding night and demanded twenty dollars for their first lovemaking encounter.

In his highly aroused state, he readily agreed.

This scenario was repeated each time they made love for the next thirty years. He enjoyed the game and thought it was a cute way for her to buy new clothes and other incidentals.

One day, she came home and found her husband in a very drunken state. During the next few minutes he related to her the ravages of financial ruin caused by corporate staff reduction and its effects on their family income.

Calmly, she handed him a bankbook showing deposits and interest for the past number of years totaling nearly one million dollars.

Pointing across the parking lot she gestured toward the local bank while handing him stock certificates worth nearly two million dollars and informing him that he was the largest stockholder in the bank.

She reminded him that for the past thirty years she had charged him each time they had sex, and this was the result of her investments.

By now he was distraught and beating his head against the side of the car.

She asked him why the disappointment at such good news and he replied, "If I had known what you were doing, I would have given you all of my business."

Hardware

Tim was fixing a door and discovered that he needed a new hinge, so he sent his blonde wife, Marianne to the hardware store.

At the hardware store Marianne saw a beautiful tea pot on a top shelf while she was waiting for Irv, the manager, to finish waiting on a customer.

When Irv was finished with his customer, Marianne asked how much for the teapot.

He replied, "That tea pot is solid silver and it costs a hundred and fifty bucks."

"That sure is a lot of money for a tea pot." Marianne exclaimed.

Then she proceeded to describe the hinge that Tim had sent her to buy, and Irv went to the backroom to find it.

From the backroom he yelled, "Marianne, you wanna screw for that hinge?"

Marianne replied, "No, but I will for the tea pot."

167

Remarry

A doctor and his young wife were sitting at dinner one evening discussing the death of a patient about their own age. After some thought, the wife asked her husband if he would remarry if she would die.

Without hesitation he replied, "Sure I would, honey. You know I don't do well on my own."

"I wouldn't want you to be lonely," replied the wife. "I guess that's all right."

After a few more minutes of contemplation she asked, "So if you were to remarry, would you live in this same house with your new wife?"

"Now that's a silly question," replied the husband. "You know how long it took us to find a suitable house close to the hospital."

She then asked, "Would you sleep in our bed with her?"

"With my back problem why would I even think of getting a different bed?"

She was beginning to feel a bit uncomfortable and asked, "Would you let her wear my mink coat?"

He replied curtly, "I paid nine grand for that coat. I sure would not let it collect dust in the closet."

"Surely you would not let her use my golf clubs?"

Without hesitating, he replied, "Of course not, she's left-handed."

Oops!

Marital Advice

A man is having difficulties with his wife and goes to the priest for advice.

"Father, something terrible is happening and I have to talk to you about it."

The priest asked, what's wrong?"

The man replied, "My wife is poisoning me."

The priest is very surprised by this and asked, "How can that be?"

The man continued, "I'm telling you, I am certain she is poisoning me. What should I do?"

The priest said, "Let me talk to her, I will see what I can find out and let you know."

A week later the priest called the man and said, "I spoke to your wife on the phone for three hours. Do you want to hear my advice?"

The man anxiously said, "Yes, of course I would."

The priest said, "Take the poison."

In-Laws

One bright, Sunday morning, everyone in a tiny town woke up early and went to church. Before the service started, everyone was sitting in their pews whispering about local things and the latest gossip.

Suddenly, at the altar, Satan appears.

Everyone starts screaming and running for the front entrance, trampling each other in their determined efforts to get away from the leering Lucifer.

Everyone evacuated the church except for one man, who sits calmly in his pew, seemingly oblivious to the fact that Evil Incarnate stands before him.

This confuses Satan a bit and he asks, "Hey, don't you know who I am?"

The man says, "Yep, sure do."

Satan says, "Well, aren't you afraid of me?"

The man says, "Nope, sure ain't afraid."

Satan is upset and says, "And why aren't you afraid of me?"

"I have been married to your sister for the past twenty years."

Children

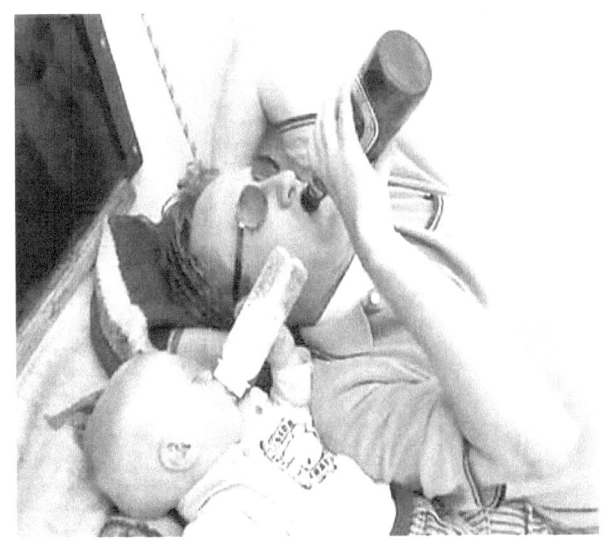

New Fathers

Four expectant fathers were in a hospital waiting room, while their wives were in labor.

The nurse arrived and announced to the first man, "Congratulations sir, you are the father of twins."

"What a coincidence," the man said with pride. "I work for the Double Time Construction Company."

The nurse returned a while later and turned to the second man, "You sir, are the father of triplets."

"Wow, that is really an incredible coincidence. I work for the 3M Corporation." My buddies at work will never let me live this one down."

An hour later, while the other two men were passing cigars around, the nurse came back. This time she turned to the third man, who had been quiet in the corner. She announced that his wife had just given birth to quadruplets.

He sat there stunned and just looked at her.

"Don't tell me, is it another coincidence?" asked the nurse.

After regaining his composure, he said, "Yes it is and I don't believe it. I work for the Four Seasons Hotel."

After hearing this, everybody's attention turned to the fourth guy, who fainted and was laying on the floor.

The nurse rushed to his side and after some time, he slowly gained consciousness.

When he was finally able to speak, they heard him whispering the same phrase over and over again. "I should have never taken that job at 7-Up, I should have never taken that job at 7-Up."

All That Glitters

A woman was due for an appointment with her gynecologist. Early one morning she received a call from the doctor's office telling her that her appointment had been rescheduled for early that morning.

She had just packed everyone off to work and school, and it was getting late. The trip to his office took a while so she didn't have any time to spare.

She rushed to the bathroom, threw off her dressing gown, wet the washcloth that was sitting next to the sink, and gave her privates a quick wash to make sure she was presentable. She threw the washcloth in the clothes basket, put on her clothes, hopped in the car, and raced to doctor's office for her appointment.

She was in the waiting room only a few minutes when she was called in. She hopped up on the table, looked over at the other side of the room and pretended to be a million miles away.

She was a bit surprised when the doctor said, "My, we have made an extra effort this morning, haven't we?"

She thought it was a bit odd, but said nothing. When the appointment was over, she heaved a sigh of relief and went home. The rest of the day was normal, with shopping, cleaning, cooking, etc.

After school, her young daughter was playing and she called out from the bathroom, "Mom, where is my washcloth?"

The woman told her to get a fresh one. The daughter said, "No, I need the one that was here by the sink. It had all my sparkles and glitters in it."

Labor Pains

A married couple went to the hospital to have their baby delivered.

Upon arriving at the hospital, they met with their doctor, who said he had invented a new machine that could transfer a portion of the mother's labor pain to the father of the baby. He asked if they were willing to try it out.

They were both very much in favor of it.

The doctor rolled in the machine, hooked it up, and set the pain transfer dial to ten percent for starters. He explained that even ten percent was probably more pain than the father had ever experienced before.

As the labor progressed, the husband felt fine and asked the doctor to go ahead and bump it up a notch.

The doctor adjusted the machine to twenty percent pain transfer.

The husband was still feeling fine. The doctor checked the husband's blood pressure and was amazed at how well he was doing.

They decided to try for fifty percent.

The husband continued to feel quite well, and since it was obviously helping out his wife considerably, the husband encouraged the doctor to transfer all the pain to him.

The wife delivered a healthy baby with virtually no pain. She and her husband were delighted with the results.

When they arrived home, they found the mailman dead on their porch.

Delivery

In the back woods of Arkansas, Don's wife went into labor in the middle of the night, and the doctor was called out to assist in the delivery.

To keep the nervous father-to-be busy, the doctor handed him a lantern and said, "Here, you hold this high so I can see what I am doing."

Soon, a beautiful baby boy was brought into the world.

"Whoa there Don," said the doctor. "Don't be in a rush to put the lantern down. I think there's yet another little one to come."

Sure enough, within minutes he had delivered another little baby.

"No, no, don't be in a great hurry to put down that lantern, young man. It seems there's yet another one."

The new father scratched his head in bewilderment, and asked the doctor, "Do you think it's the light that's attracting them?"

Texas Baby

A Texan is drinking in a New York bar when he gets a call on his cell phone.

He is grinning from ear to ear as he hangs up. He orders a round of drinks for everybody in the bar as he announces that his wife has just produced a typical Texas baby boy weighing twenty five pounds.

Nobody can believe that any new baby can weigh in at twenty five pounds, but the Texan just shrugs, "That's about average down home, folks. Like I said, my boy's a typical Texas baby boy."

Congratulations showered him from all around. One woman actually fainted due to sympathy pains.

Two weeks later he returns to the bar. The bartender says, "Say, you're the father of that typical Texas baby that weighed twenty five pounds at birth. Everybody's been making bets about how big he would be in two weeks. We were even going to call you. How much does he weigh now?"

The proud father answers, "Seventeen pounds."

The bartender is puzzled. "What happened? He weighed twenty five pounds the day he was born."

The Texas father takes a slow swig from his long-neck beer, wipes his lips on his shirt sleeve, leans toward the bartender, and proudly says, "Had him circumcised."

New Baby

With all the new technology regarding fertility, a sixty five year-old woman gave birth to a baby. When she was discharged from the hospital and went home, her relatives came to visit.

"May we see the new baby?" one asked.

"Not yet," said the sixty five year-old mother, "Soon."

Thirty minutes had passed, and another relative asked, "May we see the new baby now?"

"Not yct," said the mother.

After another few minutes had elapsed, they asked again, "May we see the baby now?"

"No," replied the mother.

Growing very impatient, they asked, "Well, when can we see the baby?"

"When it cries," she told them.

"When it cries?" they demanded. "Why do we have to wait until it cries?"

"Because, I forgot where I put the darling thing."

Mommy Test

A woman was out walking with her four year old daughter. The daughter picked up something off the ground and started to put it in her mouth.

The mother took the item away from her and told her not to do that.

"Why?" the daughter asked.

The mother said, "Because it's been lying outside, you don't know where it has been, it is very dirty and probably has germs."

At this point, the daughter looked at her mother with total admiration and asked, "How do you know all this stuff?"

The mother was thinking quickly, "All moms know this stuff. It's on the mommy test. You have to know it, or they don't let you be a mommy."

They walked along in silence for a few minutes, but she was evidently pondering this new information.

"Oh, I get it," she beamed. "So if you don't pass the test you have to be the daddy."

"Exactly," the proud mother replied, with a smile on her face and joy in her heart.

Mom Taught Me

Mom taught me RELIGION:
"You better pray that will come out of the carpet."

Mom taught me about TIME TRAVEL:
"If you don't straighten up, I'm going to knock you into the middle of next week."

Mom taught me LOGIC:
"Because I said so, that's why."

Mom taught me to PLAN AHEAD:
"Wear clean underwear in case you are in an accident."

Mom taught me IRONY:
"Keep laughing and I'll give you something to cry about."

Mom taught me about the science of OSMOSIS:
"Shut your mouth and eat your supper."

Mom taught me about CONTORTIONISM:
"Will you look at the dirt on the back of your neck."

Mom taught me about STAMINA:
"You sit there until all that spinach is finished."

Mom taught me about HYPOCRISY:
"If I told you once, I told you a million times, don't exaggerate."

Mom taught me about BEHAVIOR MODIFICATION:
"Stop acting like your father."

Mom taught me about ENVY:
"There are millions of less fortunate children in this world who don't have wonderful parents like you do."

And most of all, Mom taught me the CIRCLE OF LIFE:
"I brought you into this world and I can take you out."

Gratitude

A German sausage maker came to this country to start his own sausage factory. He did all of the work himself. He bought breeders and raised his own pigs.

He slaughtered the pigs, seasoned them, put them into the machine and they came out sausages. As the sausages came out, he tied them, boxed them, loaded them into his truck, and took them to the market to sell.

He managed to do very well for his family and even managed to put his son through college with the money he earned.

The son came home from college ready to take on the world. He derided his father for working so hard making sausages.

He said, "Dad, I have been gone for four years to college and when I get home, I notice that you have the same old truck, same old factory, same old clothes, and live in the same old house."

His father replied, "Son, it was because I have all of these same things that I could afford the expenses to put you through college."

The son said, "That's just the problem, dad. You work very hard and just put in a pig and it comes out a sausage. Wouldn't it be great if you had a device that you could put in a sausage and out came a pig?"

The old man looked at his progeny and said, "Son, if you knew where you came from you would know that I don't have a machine like that, but your mother does."

Code Words

A husband and wife decided they needed to use a code to indicate that they wanted to have sex, without letting their children in on it.

They decided to use the word typewriter.

One day the husband tells his five year old daughter, "Go tell your mommy that daddy needs to type a letter."

The child tells her mom what her dad said and her mother responds, "Tell your daddy that he can't type a letter right now, because there's a red ribbon in the typewriter."

The child went back to tell her father what mommy had said.

A few days later the mom told the daughter, "Tell daddy that he can type that letter now."

The child tells her father, waits for an answer and returns to her mother and announces, "Daddy says he doesn't need the typewriter, he already wrote the letter by hand."

The Nose Trick

A guy is tossing peanuts into the air and catching them in his mouth. In the middle of catching one, his wife asks him a question, and as he turns to answer, the peanut falls into his ear.

He tries to dig it out, but that only pushes it in deeper, so he and his wife decide the best thing to do is go to the hospital.

Just as they are about to go out the door, their daughter returns home with her date.

The parents explain the problem and the daughter's date says, "I know a trick that will get that peanut out."

He tells the father to sit down, shoves two fingers into the father's nose, and tells him to blow hard. The father blows and the peanut flies out of his ear.

The mother and daughter are all excited and thank him profusely, but the daughter's date says, "Oh, it was nothing really."

After her daughter takes her date to the kitchen for something to eat, the mother turns to the father and says, "What a clever young man. I wonder if our daughter enjoyed her date with him."

The father replies, "From the smell of his fingers I would say she did."

Dixie Wrecked

My son has a habit of leaving notes for me on the refrigerator. One morning I came downstairs to find a note that read, "My Dixie wrecked."

I read it a few times, but whatever it meant refused to sink in.

I tried putting it out of my mind but it kept coming back. "My Dixie wrecked", "My Dixie Wrecked".

Weird how that puzzling note refused to leave my awareness. It would go quietly to the back of my mind and play over and over but never would it leave. I'd bring it to the front of my attention and review it closely: "My Dixie Wrecked". Hmmm.

I got up for coffee and muttered to myself, "My Dixie wrecked." I wonder what that means?

I even said it out loud a few times, "My Dixie wrecked." What's the meaning of that?

I even asked my mom. I said to her, "My Dixie wrecked. What does that mean?"

I tried to change the accents, "y-DIXIE-Wrecked. MY-dixie-wrecked. my- dixie-WRECKED.

It was driving me nuts.

My son finally got home from school and I blurted out, "My Dick's Erect. What the hell does that mean?"

My son is such a creep.

Out of the Mouths of Babes

HOW DO YOU DECIDE WHOM TO MARRY?

You got to find somebody who likes the same stuff. Like, if you like sports, she should like it that you like sports, and she should keep the chips and dip coming. * Alan

No person really decides before they grow up who they are going to marry. God decides it all way before, and you get to find out later who you are stuck with. * Kirsten

WHAT IS THE RIGHT AGE TO GET MARRIED?

Twenty-three is the best age because you know the person forever by then. * Camille

HOW CAN A STRANGER TELL IF TWO PEOPLE ARE MARRIED?

You might have to guess, based on whether they seem to be yelling at the same kids. * Derrick

WHAT DO MOST PEOPLE DO ON A DATE?

Dates are for having fun, and people should use them to get to know each other. Even boys have something to say if you listen long enough. * Lynnette

On the first date, they just tell each other lies, and that usually gets them interested enough to go for a second date. * Martin

WHAT WOULD YOU DO ON A FIRST DATE THAT WAS TURNING SOUR?

I would run home and play dead. The next day I would call all the newspapers and make sure they wrote about me in all the dead columns. * Craig

WHAT DO YOU THINK YOUR MOM AND DAD HAVE IN COMMON?

Both don't want any more kids. * Lori

WHEN IS IT OKAY TO KISS SOMEONE?

When they are rich. * Pam

The law says you have to be eighteen, so I wouldn't want to mess with that. * Curtis

The rule goes like this: If you kiss someone, then you should marry them and have kids with them. It's the right thing to do. * Howard

Daughter Dating Rules

Rule One: If you pull into my driveway and honk you better be delivering a package, because you are sure not picking anything up.

Rule Two: You do not touch my daughter in front of me. You may glance at her, so long as you do not peer at anything below her neck. If you cannot keep your eyes or hands off of my daughter's body, I will remove them.

Rule Three: I am aware that it is considered fashionable for boys of your age to wear their trousers so loosely that they appear to be falling off their hips. Please do not take this as an insult, but you and all of your friends are complete idiots. Still, I want to be fair and open minded about this issue, so I propose a compromise. You may come to the door with your underwear showing and your pants ten sizes too big, and I will not object. However, In order to ensure that your clothes do not come off during the course of your date with my daughter, I will take my electric staple gun and fasten your trousers securely to your waist.

Rule Four: I am sure you have been told that in today's world, sex without utilizing protection of some kind can kill you. Let me explain that when it comes to sex, I am her protection, and I will kill you.

Rule Five: In order for us to get to know each other, we might talk about sports, politics, and other issues of the day. Please do not do this. The only information I require from you is an indication of when you expect to have my daughter safely back at my house, and the only word I need from you on this subject is 'early'.

Rule Six: I have no doubt you are a popular fellow, with many opportunities to date other girls. This is fine with me as long as it is okay with my daughter. Otherwise, once you have gone out with my little girl, you will continue to date no one but her until she is finished with you. If you make her cry, I will make you cry.

Rule Seven: As you stand in my front hallway waiting for my daughter to appear, and more than an hour goes by, do not sigh and fidget. If you want to be on time for the movie, you should not be dating. My daughter is putting on her makeup, a process that can take longer than painting the Golden Gate Bridge. Instead of just standing there, you can do something useful, like changing the oil in my car.

Rule Eight: The following places are not appropriate for a date with my daughter: Places where there are beds, sofas, or anything softer than a wooden stool; Places where there are no parents, policemen, or nuns within eyesight; Places where there is darkness; Places where there is dancing or holding hands; Places where the ambient temperature is warm enough to induce my daughter to wear shorts, tank tops, midriff T-shirts, or anything other than overalls, a sweater, and a goose down parka zipped up to her throat. Movies with a strong romantic or sexual theme are to be avoided, but movies which feature chainsaws are good. Hockey and football games are fine.

Rule Nine: Do not lie to me. I may appear to be a pot-bellied, balding, middle-aged, dim-witted has-been, but on issues relating to my daughter, I am the all-knowing, merciless god of your universe. If I ask you where you are going and with whom, you have one chance to tell me the truth, the whole truth and nothing but the truth. I have a shotgun, a shovel, and five acres behind the house.

Rule Ten: Be afraid. Be very afraid. It takes very little for me to mistake the sound of your car in the driveway for a chopper coming in over a rice paddy outside of Hanoi. When my Agent Orange starts acting up, the voices in my head frequently tell me to clean the guns as I wait for you to bring my daughter home. As soon as you pull into the driveway you should exit your car with both hands in plain sight. Speak the perimeter password, announce in a clear voice that you have brought my daughter home early and safely, and then return to your car. There is no need for you to come inside. The camouflaged face at the window is mine.

Children's Questions

A young boy asks his father, "Dad, is it OK for us guys to notice all the different kinds of boobs?"

The father answers, "Sure son, we would not be normal if we didn't. There are all kinds of breasts. Many depend on a woman's age.

In her twenties, a woman's breasts are like melons, round and firm.

In her thirties to forties, they are like pears, still nice but hanging a bit.

After fifty, they are like onions."

"Onions?"

"Yes, you see them and they make you cry."

Not to be outdone, his sister asks her mother, "Mom, how many kinds of thingies are there?"

The mother was delighted to have equal time and answers, "Well, daughter, a man goes through three phases.

In a man's twenties, his thingy is like a big oak, mighty and hard.

In his thirties and forties, it is like a birch, flexible, but reliable.

After his fifties, it is like a Christmas tree."

"A Christmas tree?"

"Yes. All dried up and the balls are only there for decoration."

Advice for Daughters

Do not believe you can change a man - unless he is in diapers.

What to do if your boyfriend walks out - Shut the door.

Never let your man's mind wander - it is too little to be out alone.

Go for younger men, you might as well, because they never mature anyway.

Men are all the same - they just have different faces, so that you can tell them apart.

Women do not make fools of men - most of them are the do-it-yourself types.

Best way to get a man to do something is to suggest he is too old for it.

Love is blind - Marriage is a real eye-opener.

Want a committed man - Look in a mental hospital.

The children of Israel wandered around the desert for forty years. Even in biblical times, men would not ask for directions.

If he asks what sort of books you are interested in, tell him checkbooks.

A sense of humor does not mean that you tell him jokes; it means that you laugh at his.

My Son at the Bank

A mother took her young son with her to the bank. They were in line behind a very obese woman.

As the mother patiently waited, the son looked at the woman in front of him and said, "Hey mom, she's really fat."

The woman looked at the little boy, made eye contact with his mother, and gave an understanding smile.

The boy received a reprimand from his mother.

After a few more minutes, he spread his hands as far as he could and loudly said, "Her butt is 'this' wide."

At this the woman glared at the boy and his mother severely scolded him.

After a few more minutes the boy stated loudly, "Look how the fat hangs over her belt."

The woman turned and told his mother to control her child.

This time his mother threatened him with severe bodily harm.

A few moments later, the woman's cell phone began to ring.

The young lad yelled in a panic, "Run for your life, she's backing up."

Twins

There once was a brother and a sister, fraternal twins, who were approaching their high school graduation. It was getting near prom night and neither of them had a date for it.

One day, the girl approaches her brother and says, "Hey, do you have a date for the prom yet?"

He says "No, why? Do you have someone lined up for me?"

"You might say that. Why don't you take me to the prom?"

"Take you? Are you kidding? You're my sister!"

"Are you taking somebody else out?"

"I just told you that I don't have a date."

"And neither do I, but we both want to go to the prom, don't we?"

Her brother nods. She continues, "So we should go with each other."

The brother can't see anything wrong with her reasoning, so he tells his sister that if neither of them has a date by Wednesday evening, he will take her to the prom.

Wednesday evening rolls around. Neither of the siblings has a date, so the brother tells his sister that he will take her to the prom on Friday.

At the prom, both of them have a good time. The brother is glad that his sister talked him into taking her.

Then, while he is standing at the punch bowl, his sister comes up to him again and says, "Hey, brother, let's dance."

He looks around to make sure that nobody heard her. "Look, sis, this is the Senior Prom. I am not going to dance with my own sister at the prom."

"Don't be so shy. Look, Jimmy is dancing with his cousin. So why can't you dance with your sister?"

"Oh, OK."

So they dance to a slow number. The rest of the prom passes by and after a while it's over and time to go. Both of them had a good time.

In the car, with the brother at the wheel, the sister looks over at him and says, "Let's not go straight home."

He gives her a curious look and says, "What are we going to do instead?"

"Oh, I don't know. Just drive around."

He agrees, and after they have driven around a while, out in the country, she looks over at him again and says, "Want to find some place to park?"

"Hell," he says, "Are you crazy? You are my sister, I am not going parking with you!"

"Who said anything about 'going parking'? Let's just pull over somewhere and talk for a while. It has been a busy year for both of us. How long has it been since we have had a chance to talk to each other?"

She finally talks her brother into pulling the car over on a secluded back road, and after a few minutes of idle talk, she looks over at him again.

"Hey, why don't you kiss me?" she says.

"You have been suggesting a lot of weird things lately, do you know that? I am not going to kiss you, you are my sister!" He reached for the key to start the car.

She reached out and took his hand. "I know I'm your sister. You have mentioned that a lot lately. You are my brother, and don't we love each other? Why shouldn't we kiss if we feel like it?" She kissed him on the cheek and he finally kissed her back. After a few minutes of kissing, she whispered in his ear, "Come on. Let's do it."

"Do what," said her brother, but he had a good idea of what his sister had in mind.

"You know what," his sister replied.

"I can't do that with you, you are my. . ." His voice trailed off.

While he was on top of her, his sister murmured, "You know, you are a lot lighter than dad."

"I know," said her brother. "Mom told me."

Getting Ahead

A man is waiting for his wife to give birth. The doctor comes in and informs the dad that his son was born without torso, arms, or legs. The son is just a head.

The parents love their son and raise him as well as they can, with love and compassion.

After twenty one years, the son is now old enough for his first drink. Dad takes him to the bar, tells his son that he is proud of him, and orders up the biggest, strongest drink for his boy.

The bartender and the other bar patrons watch as the boy takes his first sip of alcohol.

Thwap! A torso pops out.

The shocked father asks his son to try another drink.

The patrons chant, "Take another drink."

Thwap! Two arms and hands pop out.

The crowd goes wild. The father is crying and wailing and begs his son on to drink again.

By now the boy is getting tipsy, but with his new hands he reaches down, grabs his drink, and guzzles the last of it.

Thwap! Two legs and feet pop out.

The place is in chaos. The father falls to his knees and thanks God.

The boy stands up on his new legs and stumbles to the left, then to the right and through the front door into the street, where a truck runs over him and kills him instantly.

The group falls silent. The father moans. The bartender says, "He should have quit drinking while he was still a head."

Son Helps

An old man lived alone in Ireland. He wanted to spade his potato garden, but it was very hard work.

His only son, who would have helped him, was in prison.

The old man wrote a letter to his son and mentioned his difficulty with turning over the potato garden.

Shortly, he received this reply, "For Heaven's sake, dad, do not dig up that garden, that's where I buried the guns. I will take care of it for you when I get out."

Before daybreak the next morning, a dozen soldiers showed up and dug up the entire garden, without finding any guns.

The old man was a bit confused and wrote another letter to his son, telling him what happened, and asking him what to do next.

His son's reply was, "Plant your potatoes, dad. It was the best I could do for you."

Family Secret

A man and his wife were about to celebrate fifty years together. Their three very successful and wealthy children agreed to a Sunday dinner in honor of their parents. As usual, they were all late and had a varied assortment of excuses.

"Happy anniversary, mom and dad," gushed son number one, "Sorry, I'm running late. I had an emergency, you know how it is, didn't have time to get you both a present."

"Not to worry. The important thing is that we are all together today," said the dad.

Son number two arrived and announced, "You and mom still look great, dad. Just flew in from L. A. and didn't have time to get you a present. I am very sorry."

"It's nothing, glad you are able to be here," said the father.

The daughter arrived. "Hello to you both. Happy Anniversary! I'm sorry, but my boss is sending me out of town and I was really busy packing, so I didn't have time to get you guys anything."

The father said, "I really don't care, at least the five of us are together today."

During dinner, the father put down his knife and fork, looked up, and said, "Listen you three, there is something your mother and I have wanted to tell you for a long time. Your mother and I came to this country penniless and desperate. Despite this, we were able to raise each of you and send you to college. We always knew we loved each other but we never found the time to get married."

The three kids gasped in unison, "You mean we are bastards?"

"Yes, and cheap ones too." said the dad.

Boy Tricks

One day in the backwoods, Terrible Tommy was walking to school with his girlfriend.

He thought he would impress her and said, "I bet you I can push my father's outhouse into the river."

She didn't think he could, but he took a running start, rammed into the outhouse, and knocked it into the river. The young girl was very impressed and walked the rest of the way to school hand in hand with Tommy.

That day at school, they studied the story about George Washington and the cherry tree, learning the moral to never tell a lie.

Tommy went home after school and when he walked in the door, his father was waiting for him.

He said, "Son, did you push my outhouse into the river?"

Tommy said, "Dad, I want to be like George Washington and never lie. Yes, I did."

His dad spanked him from one end of the house to the other.

After Tommy was finished sobbing, he asked his father, "Dad, why did you whip me? I didn't lie. George Washington cut down the cherry tree and didn't lie about it, and he didn't get a whipping."

Tommy's dad looked at him and said, "George Washington's dad wasn't sitting in that cherry tree when he cut it down."

Bus Riding

A husband and wife are waiting at the bus stop with their nine children.

A blind man joins them after a few minutes. When the bus arrives, they find it overloaded and only the wife and nine children are able to fit on the bus.

So the husband and the blind man decide to walk. After a while, the husband gets irritated by the ticking of the stick of the blind man as he taps it on the sidewalk, and says to him, "Why don't you put a piece of rubber at the end of your stick? That ticking sound is driving me crazy."

The blind man replies, "If you would have put a rubber at the end of your stick, we would be riding the bus, so shut up."

Triplets

A pregnant woman with triplets was walking down the street, when a masked robber runs out of a bank and shoots her three times in the stomach.

Luckily the babies are okay. The surgeon decides to leave bullets in, because it was too risky to operate. The woman had two healthy girls and a healthy boy.

All went fine for sixteen years, until one day, one of the daughters busted in her room in tears.

"What's wrong?" asks the mother.

"I was taking a pee, and this bullet came out," replied the daughter.

The mother tells her that it is fine, and explains to her what had happened sixteen years ago.

A week later, the second daughter runs into her room in tears. "Mom, I was taking a pee, and this bullet came out."

Again the mother tells the second daughter not to worry and explains what had happened sixteen years ago.

A week later, her son came into her room in tears.

"Its OK," says mom. "I know what happened. You were taking a pee, and a bullet came out."

"No," says the boy. "I was playing with myself, and I shot the dog.

Using Condoms

A father and his little boy, Tommy, went into a local drugstore to pick up a prescription. While in the store, the little boy was browsing around and came upon a rather large display for condoms. The little boy was amused by all the brightly colored packages and the different types and quantities.

Then Tommy finds his father and asks him, "Daddy, what are all those condoms for?"

The father stutters a bit and says, "Well, they are for protection, son. Protection from diseases when a man and a woman make love."

Tommy contemplated the concept for a few moments and then asks, "Then why do these come in a package of three?"

The father answers, "Those are for young men in high school. One each for Friday night, Saturday night, and Sunday afternoon."

Tommy asks, "Well then, why are these in packages of six?"

His father replies, "Those are for young men in college. There are two for Friday night, two for Saturday, and two Sunday afternoon."

"Wow," says Tommy in amazement and he asks, "Why are these packaged a dozen at a time?"

The father answers, "Those are for married men. One for January, one for February. . ."

Light a Candle

The priest stood at the church door greeting the parishioners after mass. "Good mornin' to ya Mr. and Mrs. O'Riley. I married you ten years ago, but I never see any of your children in church."

"Deed you did, father. We've not been blessed. My husband and I have tried but we have not been successful," said Mrs. O'Riley.

"I'm going to Rome for a sabbatical. I will light a candle for you in the great cathedral at the Vatican. Perhaps the Holy Mother will look kindly on you and your husband."

Several years later, back at the church door, the priest is greeting and meets Mrs. O'Riley.

"Mrs. O'Riley, did you ever have any children?"

"Deed I did, Father," she said pointing to a family behind her. "We've had a set of triplets, a set of twins, and two singles since we last saw you."

"Praise be the Holy Mother. She's blessed you, but I don't see Mr. O'Riley. Is he here?"

"No. He's gone to Rome to blow out your damn candle."

A Child's Prayers

A father put his three year old daughter to bed, told her a story, and listened to her prayers which she ended by saying, "God bless mommy, God bless daddy, God bless grandma, and good-bye grandpa."

The father asked, "Why did you say good-bye grandpa?"

The little girl said, "I don't know daddy, it just seemed like the thing to do."

The next day grandpa died.

The father thought it was a strange coincidence. A few months later the father put his girl to bed and listened to her prayers, which she ended by saying, "God bless mommy, God Bless daddy and good-bye grandma."

This seemed like an odd thing for her to say, but the father remained quiet.

The next day the grandmother died.

Oh my, thought the father, my little girl is in contact with the other side.

Several weeks later when the girl was going to bed the dad heard her say, "God bless mommy and good-bye daddy."

He practically went into shock.

He couldn't sleep all night and got up at the crack of dawn to go to his office. He was nervous all day. He had lunch sent in and watched the clock. He figured if he could just get by until midnight he would be okay.

He felt safe in the office, so instead of going home at the end of the day he stayed there, drinking coffee, looking at his watch, and jumping at every sound.

Finally midnight arrived and he breathed a sigh of relief and went home. When he got home his wife said, "I have never seen you work so late, what's the matter?"

He said, "I don't want to discuss it, I just had the worst day of my life."

She said, "You think you had a bad day, you will never believe what happened here. This morning the milkman dropped dead on our front porch."

Letter from School

Dear Dad,

$chool i$ really great. I am making lot$ of friend$ and $tudying very hard.

With all my $tuff, I $imply can't think of anything I need, $o if you would like, you can ju$t $end me a card, a$ I would love to hear from you.

Love,
Your $on.

✐ ✐ ✐ ✐

Dear Son,

I kNOw that astroNOmy, ecoNOmics, and oceaNOgraphy are eNOugh to keep even an hoNOr student busy.

Do NOt forget that the pursuit of kNOwledge is a NOble task, and you can never study eNOugh.

Love,
Dad

Gifts for Mom

Three sons left home, went out on their own, and prospered. They got back together and discussed the gifts they were able to give their elderly mother.

The first said, "I built a big house for our mother."

The second said, "I sent her a Mercedes with a driver."

The third smiled and said, "I have you both beat. You know how mom loves the Bible, and you know she can't see very well, I sent her a parrot that can recite the entire Bible.

It took twenty monks in a monastery twelve years to teach him. I had to contribute a hundred grand a year for twelve years, but it was worth it. Mom just has to name the chapter and verse and the parrot will recite it."

Soon thereafter, mom sent out her letters of thanks to her three fine children.

"Jim," she wrote the first son, "The house you built is huge. I live in only one room, but I have to clean the whole house."

"John," she wrote, "I am too old to travel. I stay home all the time, so I never use the Mercedes and the driver is very rude."

"Dearest Joseph," she wrote to her third son, "You were the only son to have the good sense to know what your mother likes. That chicken was delicious."

Phone Call

The phone rings and Tommy picks it up, "Hello?"

"Hi, this is daddy. Is mommy near the phone?"

"No daddy. She is upstairs in the bedroom with Uncle Mike."

After a brief pause, he says, "But you don't have an Uncle Mike."

"Yes I do, and he is upstairs in the bedroom with mommy."

"OK, this is what I want you to do. Put the phone down, run upstairs, knock on the bedroom door, and shout to mommy that daddy's car just pulled into the driveway."

"OK daddy, just a minute."

A few minutes later Tommy comes back to the phone. "I did it daddy."

"And what happened?"

"Well, mommy got all scared, jumped out of bed with no clothes on, and ran around screaming. Then she tripped on the rug, hit her head on the dresser, and now she isn't moving at all."

"Oh my God, what about Uncle Mike?"

"He jumped out of the bed with no clothes on too. He was all scared and jumped out of the back window into the swimming pool, but I guess he didn't know that you took out the water last week to clean it.

He hit the bottom of the pool and I think he's dead."

There is a long pause and finally the man asks, "Swimming pool? Is this 555-5678?"

Business Trips

A businessman returned home from a trip at the same time a storm hit with crashing thunder and severe lightning.

When the man went into his bedroom about midnight, he found his two children in bed with his wife. They were apparently afraid of the loud storm. He resigned himself to sleep in the guest bedroom that night.

The next day, he talked to the children, and explained that it was OK to sleep with their mom when the storm was bad, but when he was expected home, they shouldn't sleep with their mother on that night.

They understood what he was saying and agreed.

After his next trip a few weeks later, his wife and the children went to pick him up at the appointed time.

His plane was late, so his family went into the terminal to wait for his plane's arrival. In the terminal were hundreds of other families and loved ones also waiting for their arriving passengers.

As the man entered the waiting area, his son saw him and came running and shouted, "Hi, dad. I have got some good news."

The man waved back and said, "What's the good news, son?"

The lad replied, "Nobody slept with mommy while you were away this time."

The terminal became very quiet, as everyone in the waiting area looked at the little boy, then turned to him, and then searched the rest of the area to see if they could figure out exactly who the boy's mother was.

Heads Up

A woman is in the delivery room in labor. One final push and the baby came out. Above the baby's muffled first cries, she hears the horrified gasps of the doctor and shrieks of the nurses. The baby is rushed away before she can see it.

Later, a doctor comes in and says, "I am afraid there is a serious problem with your new son. It seems he was born without a body."

She stammers, "You mean. . ."

"Yes," the doctor says, "He is just a head, but on the bright side, he is a perfectly healthy and normal head."

The years pass by, and the mother takes to putting her son on a table upstairs near the window so he can look outside at the beautiful scenery.

One day, the phone rings. It's the hospital. A surgeon informs the woman that there has been a horrible accident, and a young man has been completely decapitated. There is a good chance that her son's head can be attached to the victim's body.

She drops the phone, runs upstairs to where her son has rested most of his life and says, "Son, I have the most wonderful surprise for you."

The child looks up at his mother and replies, "I hope it's not another hat."

College Letter

Dear mom and dad,

It has been almost six months since I left for college and I suppose you wonder how I am doing. I'm sorry for not having written before, but I will try to cover everything with this letter.

Please sit down before you read on.

I am doing very well and the bandages should come off this month. The skull fracture and concussion that I received, when I had to jump out of the dorm window when it caught on fire, are almost completely healed. I wasn't in the hospital long. I can see clearly now almost all of the time and the headaches don't come as often as they used to.

Lucky for us that a guy was passing by and called the fire department for us. He came by to visit me in the hospital every day. When I got out, he let me live with him as I had nowhere else to go, because the dorm burned completely to the ground.

He has a cute basement room not too far from school. He is so nice and we have fallen in love and he asked me to marry him.

We are not sure when to have the wedding, but we definitely want to have it before the baby begins to show.

You are probably worried that I am pregnant, but you always wanted to be grandparents. I know that you will grow to love the baby and take care of it just as you took car of me.

The doctor assured me the baby should be fine.

Our only problem with the wedding date is the silly infection that my boy friend has, which keeps him from passing the blood test. I think that I must have caught it too, but the doctor says that penicillin shots will take care of everything.

I know that you will enjoy meeting my fiancé and welcome him into your home as he opened his up to me. He is very nice and ambitious, too. Willy doesn't have much education and is of a different religion, but I know you won't hold that against him.

I almost forgot to mention that he is of a different race, too. You always taught me to be tolerant of others so I know that this won't bother you, either. His family is rather important where he comes from. His father is the head concierge in a hotel in Botswana.

Now that I have brought you up to date on what is happening in school, there is one more little thing. There was no fire, no concussion, no wedding, no baby, no infection, and no boyfriend, but I am getting a D in Math and I am failing Chemistry. I thought this might help keep it in perspective for you.

Love

Marge

Children Quickies

John Hopkins Medical Center is reporting an unusual occurrence in the Obstetrics department:

A child was born with both male and female organs.

A penis and a brain.

While in line at the bank one afternoon, Terrible Tommy decided to release some pent-up energy and ran amok. His mother was finally able to grab hold of him after receiving looks of disgust and annoyance from other patrons.

His mother told him that if he did not start behaving he would be punished. Tommy looked her in the eye and said in a voice just as threatening, "If you don't let me go right now, I will tell Grandma that I saw you kissing daddy's pee-pee last night."

The silence was deafening. Even the tellers stopped what they were doing. His mother gathered her last bit of dignity and walked out of the bank with Tommy in tow. The last thing heard when the door closed behind them were screams of laughter.

There are three ways to get things done. Do it yourself, hire someone, or forbid your children from doing it.

A woman stood inside the front door, her arms full of coats. Four small children scurried around her. Her husband, coming down the stairs, asked why she was standing there.

"Here," she said, handing him the coats. "This time you put the children into their coats, and I'll go honk the horn."

Why did the blonde decide to have only three children?
She heard that one out of every four children born in the world was Chinese.

Real mothers know that their kitchen utensils are probably in the sandbox.

Real mothers often have sticky floors, filthy ovens, and happy kids.

Real mothers know that dried play dough does not come out of shag carpets.

Real mothers do not want to know what the vacuum just sucked up.

Real mothers sometimes ask 'why me?' and get their favorite answer when a little voice says, 'because I love you best.'

A proud new father looked at his new son, but was muttering to himself, "With those small arms, you will never be a weight lifter. With those small legs, you will never be a dancer. With those tiny eyes, you will never become a famous astronomer. Oh goodness, you will never become a porn star, either."

Where do mothers learn all the things they tell their daughters not to do?

One afternoon, Sue returned home from school and announced that a friend had explained to her where babies come from.

Her mother replied, "Why don't you tell me all about it?"

Sue explained, "Well, mommy and daddy take off all of their clothes and the daddy's thingy stands up, and then the mommy puts it in her mouth, and then it sort of explodes, and that's how you get babies."

Her mother shook her head, leaned over to meet her eye-to-eye, and said, "Oh, honey, that's very sweet, but that is not how you get babies. That is how you get jewelry."

There was a middle-aged couple that had two beautiful teenage daughters. The couple decided to try one last time for the son they always wanted. After months of trying, the wife finally became pregnant and delivered a healthy baby boy nine months later.

The joyful father rushed into the nursery to see his new son. He took one look and was horrified to see the ugliest child he had ever seen. He went to his wife and told her there was no way he could be the father of that child.

"Look at the two beautiful daughters I fathered."

Then he gave her a stern look and asked, "Have you been fooling around on me?"

The wife smiled sweetly and said, "Not this time."

Extra Curricular Activities

"Hey, Mom! You got
any more of that
hot snatch Dad
was raving about
last night?"

Confessions

Tommy Shaughnesy enters the confessional box and says, "Bless me Father, for I have sinned. I have been with a loose woman."

The priest asks, "Is that you Tommy Shaughnesy?"

"Yes, Father, it is."

And who was the woman you were with?"

"I can't be tellin' ya, Father. I don't want to ruin her reputation."

"Well, Tommy, I'm sure to find out sooner or later, so you may as well tell me now. Was it Brenda O'Malley?"

"I cannot say."

"Was it Patricia Kelly?"

"I'll never tell."

"Was it Liz Shannon?"

" I am sorry, but I'll not tell her name."

"Was it Cathy Morgan?"

"My lips are sealed."

The priest sighs in frustration. "You're a steadfast lad, Tommy Shaughnesy, and I admire that, but you have sinned, and you must atone."

He gave Tommy penance and dismissed him. Tommy walks back to his pew. His friend Sean slides over and whispers, "What did you get?"

Tommy said, "Three Our Fathers and four new leads."

Haircuts

A man stuck his head into a barbershop and asked, "How long before I can get a haircut?"

The barber looked around the shop and said, "About two hours."

The guy left.

A few days later, the same guy stuck his head in the door and asked, "How long before I can get a haircut?"

The barber looked around at the shop full of customers and said, "About two hours."

The guy left.

A week later, the same guy stuck his head in the shop and asked, "How long before I can get a haircut?"

The barber looked around the shop and said, "About an hour and a half."

The guy left.

The barber looked over at a friend in the shop and said, "Hey, Bill, follow that guy and see where he goes."

In a little while, Bill came back into the shop laughing hysterically.

The barber asked, "Where did he go when he left here?"

Bill looked up and said, "To your house."

Old Maids

Two old-maid, virgin sisters were having a conversation. Gladys looks at Betty and says, "I am not going to die a virgin. I am going out and I am not coming home until I have been laid."

Betty says, "Well, make sure you are home by ten so I don't worry about you."

10 o'clock rolls around and there's no sign of Gladys. . . 11 o'clock. . . 12 o'clock. . . Finally about fifteen minutes after one, the front door flies open. Gladys comes in and heads straight to the bathroom.

Betty goes and knocks on the door, "Are you okay, Gladys?"

No answer, so she opens the door and there sits Gladys with her panties around her ankles, legs spread, and her head stuck between her legs trying to look up herself.

"What is it, Gladys? What's wrong?" asks Betty.

"Betty, it was eight inches long when it went in and four inches when it came out. When I find the other half you are going to have the time of your life."

Dirty Talk

A woman went to a pet shop and immediately spotted a large beautiful parrot. There was a sign on the cage that said twenty-five dollars.

"Why so cheap," she asked the pet store owner.

He said, "This bird used to live in a house of prostitution, and sometimes it spouts some dirty talk."

The woman thought about this, but decided she wanted the bird anyway. She took it home, hung the bird's cage up in her living room and waited for the bird to say something.

The bird looked around the room, then at her and said, "New house, new madam."

The woman was a bit surprised at the implication, but thought, "That's not so bad."

When her teenage daughter returned from school the bird saw her and said, "New house, new madam, new girl."

The girl and the woman were surprised, but then began to laugh about the situation.

Moments later, the woman's husband, Bill, came home from work. The bird looked at him and said, "Hi Bill."

Old and Young

An older, white haired man walked into a jewelry store one Friday evening with a beautiful young girl at his side. He told the jeweler he was looking for a special ring for his girlfriend.

The jeweler looked through his stock and brought out a five thousand dollar ring and showed it to him.

The old man said, "I don't think you understand. I want something very special."

With that, the jeweler went to his special stock and brought another ring over. "Here's a stunning ring at only twenty thousand," the jeweler said.

The young lady's eyes sparkled and her whole body trembled with excitement.

The old man noticed her reaction and said, "We'll take it."

The jeweler asked how payment would be made and the old man stated, by check. "I know you need to make sure my check is good, so I will write it now and you can call the bank Monday to verify the funds. I will stop by and pick the ring up Monday afternoon," he said.

Monday morning, a very upset jeweler phoned the old man. "There is no money in that account."

The old man said, "I know, but can you imagine the weekend of fun I had?"

Diagnoses

A young doctor had moved out to a small community to replace the retiring country doctor. The older doctor suggested the young one accompany him on his rounds so the community would become used to a new doctor.

At the first house a woman complained, "I have been a little sick with an upset stomach."

The older doctor said, "You have probably been overdoing the fresh fruit. Why not cut back on the amount you have been eating and see if that does the trick?"

As they left the younger man said, "You didn't even examine that woman. How did you arrive at your diagnosis so quickly?"

"I didn't have to. You noticed I dropped my stethoscope on the floor in there? When I bent over to pick it up, I noticed a half-dozen banana peels in the trash. That was what probably was making her sick."

The younger doctor said, "Very clever. I will try that at the next house."

Arriving at the next house, they spent several minutes talking with a younger woman. She complained that she just didn't have the energy she once did. "I am feeling terribly run down lately."

"You probably have been doing too much work for the church," the younger doctor told her. "Perhaps you should cut back a bit and see if that helps."

As they left, the elder doc said, "Your diagnosis is almost certainly correct, but how did you arrive at it?"

"Just as you did at the last house, I dropped my stethoscope and when I bent down to retrieve it, I saw the preacher under the bed."

Women's Night Out

Two women go out one weekend without their husbands. They came back just before dawn. Both of them are still drunk and they felt the urge to pee.

They noticed the only place to stop was a nearby cemetery. They were scared and drunk, but they stopped and decided to go there anyway.

The first one did not have anything to clean her self with, so she took off her panties and used them to clean herself and discarded them.

The second couldn't find anything either and thought to herself, "I'm not getting rid of my panties like she did." She looked around found and used a piece of ribbon from a flower wreath to clean herself.

The two husbands were talking to each other on the phone the next morning and one says to the other, "We have to be on the look-out. It seems that our wives may have been up to no good last night. My wife came home this morning without her panties."

The other one responded, "You're lucky, mine came home with a card stuck to her ass that read, 'We will never forget you'."

Superman

A man tried to sneak into his house early one morning, only to be confronted by his wife at the front door. "Where have you been, Superman? It's 6 AM!"

"My love, remember I told you I had a meeting with those important Japanese clients?"

"Well, Superman, how late was your meeting? 9 PM? 11 PM? It's 6 in the morning."

"Ah, darling, we had to take them out for drinks."

"All right, Superman, you went drinking at 11, but the bars close at 2. Where have you been?"

"Afterward, everyone was hungry, because we skipped dinner, so we found an all night restaurant and got something to eat."

"You ate for four hours? It's 6 AM."

"Are you serious? They came halfway around the world. We wanted to show them a good time, and then I headed straight home, but there was an accident that blocked traffic so it took me three hours to get here."

"Superman, you are so busted."

"Why do you keep calling me, 'Superman'?"

"Because you are wearing your underwear over your pants."

Silk Pajamas

A man called home to his wife and said, "Honey I have been asked to go fishing up in Canada with my boss and several of his friends. We'll be gone for a week. This is good opportunity for me to get that big promotion."

He continued, "Could you please pack enough clothes for a week and set out my rod and tackle box? We will be leaving from the office and I will swing by the house to pick my things up. Oh, please pack my new blue silk pajamas."

His wife thinks this sounds a bit fishy, but being the good wife, she did exactly what her husband asked.

The following weekend he came home a little tired but otherwise looking good.

His wife welcomed him home and asked if he caught many fish?

He said, "Yes. Lots of salmon, some bluegill, and a few swordfish, but why didn't you pack my new blue silk pajamas like I asked you to do."

His wife replied, "I sure did pack them. I put them in your tackle box."

Socrates Test

In ancient Greece, Socrates was widely lauded for his wisdom. One day the great philosopher came upon an acquaintance, who said, "Socrates, do you know what I heard about one of your students?"

"Wait a moment," Socrates replied, "Before you tell me, I would like you to pass a little test. It's called the Test of Three."

"Test of Three?"

"That is correct," Socrates continued. "Before you talk to me about my student let us take a moment to test what you are going to say. The first test is Truth. Have you made absolutely sure that what you are about to tell me is true?"

"No," the man replied, "Actually, I just heard about it."

"All right," said Socrates. "So you don't really know if it's true or not. Now let's try the second test, the test of Goodness. Is what you are about to tell me about my student something good?"

"No, to the contrary."

"So, you want to tell me something bad about him even though you are not certain it is true?" The man shrugged, a little embarrassed. Socrates continued, "You may still pass though because there is a third test of Usefulness. Is what you want to tell me about my student going to be useful to me?"

"Maybe."

"Well," concluded Socrates, "If what you want to tell me is neither true, nor good, or may not be useful, why tell it to me?"

The man was defeated and ashamed and said no more. This is the reason Socrates was a great philosopher and held in such high esteem. It also explains why Socrates never found out that Plato was screwing his wife.

Chastity Belt

King Arthur was going off to fight the Holy Wars and decided that he must preserve the dignity of the queen during his absence.

He had a chastity belt made specifically for her that was constructed with a miniature guillotine. Anything that entered was immediately chopped off.

The crusades lasted much longer than the king anticipated, but he returned undaunted, knowing that the queen would be safe.

When he returned, he lined up all of the knights of the roundtable in the great hall and had them drop their pants.

As he inspected each one, he found only a stub remaining and banished each of them from his kingdom.

When he arrived at the last knight, Sir Lancelot, he found that his friend was still in good shape and he threw his arms around him and congratulated him.

The king said, "Faithful Lancelot, you are a true friend to me and I will reward you. Tell me what do you want more than anything else?"

Lancelot looked at the king and said, "Ugh blub glug glub."

Secretarial Affair

Morris came home to find his wife crying. "What's wrong, Sadie?"

Sadie replied, "Mrs. Goldberg told me you are having an affair with your secretary. Why, Morris? Haven't I been a good wife? I cooked, raised our children, and stood beside you for all these years. What haven't I done for you?"

Morris confessed, "It's true, Sadie, you are the best wife a man could hope for. You make me happy in everyway. . . but one. You don't moan when we have sex."

Sadie looked up, "If I moaned during sex, you would stop cheating on me? Let's go to the bedroom right now so I can show you how I can moan during sex."

They went to the bedroom, got undressed, and climbed between the sheets. As they kissed, Sadie asked, "Now, Morris? Should I moan now?"

"No, not yet, Sadie."

As Morris fondled Sadie, she asked, "What about now? Should I moan now?"

"No. I'll tell you when." He climbed on top of her and began intercourse.

"Now, Morris? Do you want me to moan now?"

"Wait. I'll tell you when."

Moments later, in the heat of passion, seconds before reaching climax, Morris yelled, "Now, Sadie, moan! MOAN!"

With great sincerity Sadie cried, "Oy! What a day I've had. . ."

Pest Control

A woman was having a passionate affair with an inspector from a pest-control company.

One afternoon they were carrying on in the bedroom together when her husband arrived home unexpectedly.

"Quick," said the woman to her lover, "Into the closet."

She pushed the stark naked man into the closet.

The husband heard some noise and became suspicious. He searched the whole bedroom and discovered the man in the closet.

"Who are you?" he asked the guy in the closet.

"I am an inspector from Bugs-B-Gone," said the exterminator.

"What are you doing in there?" the husband asked.

"I'm investigating a complaint about an infestation of moths," the man replied.

"And where are your clothes?" asked the husband.

The man looked down at himself and said, "Those little bastards."

Expense Account

June 1	Ad for female typist	40.00
June 3	Flowers for new typist	12.00
June 6	Weekly salary for new girl	400.00
June 8	Roses for lovely new girl	50.00
June 10	Candy for wife	10.00
June 11	Lunch for sweet new girl	80.00
June 14	Weekly salary with raise	550.00
June 16	Movie tickets for self and wife	18.00
June 18	Theater tickets for Mary and self	75.00
June 19	Ice cream for wife	6.00
June 20	Candy for Mary	25.00
June 21	Mary's new salary	800.00
June 24	Dinner and drinks for Lovely Mary	225.00
June 28	Doctor for stupid Mary	1,000.00
June 29	Fur coat for wife	2,000.00
June 30	Ad for male typist	40.00

My Wife

A guy on a date parks his car and gets the girl in the back seat. They make love one time and the girl wants it again, so the guy complies.

She wants more and they do it again. She still wants more and the guy says, "Excuse me a minute, I have to relieve myself."

While out of the car he notices a man down the street changing a flat tire. He asks the man, "Look, I have this gal in my car and I have given it to her four or five times and she still wants more. I'll change your flat tire if you take over for me."

The gentleman is kind enough to oblige and he is just getting in the high numbers when a cop knocks on the window and shines a light on them.

The cop asks, "What are you doing in there?"

The guy says, "I'm making love to my wife."

The cop asks, "Why don't you do that at home?"

The guy answers, "To tell you the truth, I didn't know it was my wife until you shined the light on her."

Hanging Around

A man went to the bar and ordered a double. He leaned over and confided to the bartender, "I am so upset."

"Oh yeh, what happened?" asked the bartender politely.

"I met this beautiful woman who invited me back to her home. We stripped off our clothes, jumped into bed and were just about to make love when her husband came in the front door. I had to jump out of the bedroom window and hang from the ledge by my fingernails."

"Gee, that was a tough situation." says the bartender.

"Right, but that's not what really got me aggravated. When her husband came into the room he said 'Hey great, you're naked already. Let me just take a leak.' And the lazy guy pissed out the window right onto my head?"

"No wonder you are in a lousy mood."

"Yeh, but I haven't told you what really, really got to me. Next, I had to listen to them grunting and groaning and when they finished, the husband tossed his condom out of the window, and it landed right on my head."

"That really is a drag." says the bartender.

"Oh, I'm not finished. See what really pissed me off was when the husband had to take a dump. It turns out that their toilet is broken, so he stuck his ass out of the window and let loose right on top of my head."

The bartender paled and replied "That would sure mess up my day."

"But do you know what really ticked me off? When I looked down and saw that I was hanging out the first floor window and my feet were only six inches off the ground."

231

Sudden Urge

Kim worked in a pickle factory. He had been employed there for a number of years when he came home one day to confess to his wife that he had a terrible compulsion. He had an extreme urge to stick his penis in the pickle slicer.

His wife suggested that he should see a therapist to talk about it, but Kim indicated that he would be too embarrassed. He vowed to overcome the compulsion on his own.

One day a few weeks later Kim came home with his head down.

His wife could see at once that something was seriously wrong. "What's wrong, Kim?" she asked.

"Do you remember that I told you how I had this tremendous urge to put my penis in the pickle slicer?"

"Oh, Kim, you didn't."

"Yes, I did."

"My God, what happened?"

"I got fired."

"No, I mean what happened with the pickle slicer?"

"Oh, she got fired too."

Infidelity

A man was returning home a day early from a business trip and got into a taxi at the airport after midnight.

While on their way to his home, he asked the cabby if he would be a witness.

The man suspected his wife was having an affair and expected to catch her in the act. The cabby agreed to be a witness if the man would pay him a hundred dollars. The man agreed.

The husband and cabby arrived at the house and quietly tiptoed into the bedroom. The husband flipped on the lights, pulled the blanket back, and there was his wife in bed with another man.

The husband put his gun to the man's head, and the wife shouted, "Don't do it! This man has been very generous. Who do you think paid for the Corvette I said I bought for you? He did. Who do you think paid for our new cabin cruiser? He did. Who do you think pays our monthly country club dues you believe I budget for? He does."

The husband, looked over at the cab driver and said, "What would you do in a case like this?"

The cabby said, "I would cover him with that blanket before he catches a cold."

One Kiss

One day a fellow noticed that a new couple had moved into the house next door. He also noticed that the woman liked to sunbathe in the backyard in a skimpy bikini that showed off a magnificent pair of breasts. He made it a point to water and trim his lawn as much as possible, hoping for more sightings.

Finally, he could stand it no more. He walked to the front door of the new neighbor's house and rang the bell. The husband, a large, burly man, opened the door.

"Excuse me," the man stammered, "I couldn't help noticing how beautiful your wife is."

"So," his hulking neighbor replied.

"I am really struck by how beautiful her breasts are. I would gladly pay you ten thousand dollars if I could kiss those breasts."

The burly guy is about to deck him when his wife appears and stops him. She pulls him inside and they discuss the offer for a few moments. They return and ask the neighbor to step inside.

The husband said, "For ten grand you can kiss my wife's breasts."

At this the wife unbuttons her blouse, and the twin objects of desire hang free at last. Our man takes one in each hand, and proceeds to rub his face against them in total ecstasy.

This goes on for several minutes, until her husband gets annoyed. "Do it, kiss them," he growled.

"I can't," replied the man, still nuzzling away.

"Why not?" demanded the husband.

"I don't have ten thousand dollars."

Priest and Nun

A priest was driving along and saw a nun on the side of the road. He stopped and offered her a lift which she accepted. She got in and crossed her legs, forcing her gown to open and reveal a lovely leg. The priest took a look and nearly had an accident.

After controlling the car, he stealthily slid his hand up her leg.

The nun looked at him and immediately said, "Father, remember Psalm 129."

The priest was flustered and apologized profusely. He forced himself to remove his hand. However, he was unable to remove his eyes from her leg.

Further on while changing gear, he let his hand slide up her leg again. The nun once again said, "Father, remember Psalm 129."

Once again the priest apologized. "Sorry sister, but the flesh is weak."

Arriving at the convent, the nun got him gave him a meaningful glance and went on her way.

On his arrival at the church, the priest rushed to retrieve a bible and looked up Psalm 129. It said, "Go forth and seek, further up you will find glory."

Rainy Day Affair

A woman was having a daytime affair while her husband was at work. One wet and lusty day she was in bed with her boyfriend when, to her horror, she heard her husband's car pull into the driveway.

"Oh my God! Hurry, grab your clothes, and jump out the window. My husband is home early."

"I can't jump out the window. It's raining out there."

"If my husband catches us in here, he will kill us both," she replied. "He has a very quick temper and a very large gun. Rain is the least of your problems."

The boyfriend falls out of bed, grabs his clothes, and jumps out the window. As he began running down the street in the pouring rain, he quickly discovered he had run right into the middle of the town's annual marathon.

He begins running along side the others. Even though he was naked, he tried to blend in as best he could. After a while, a small group of runners, who had been watching him, jogged closer.

"Do you always run in the nude?" one asked.

"Yes," he replied. "It feels so wonderfully free."

Another runner moved alongside. "Do you always run carrying your clothes under your arm?"

"Yes. That way I can get dressed at the end of the run and get in my car to go home."

A third runner cast his eyes a little lower and queried. "Do you always wear a condom when you run?"

"No, just when it's raining."

Wife's Night Out

A wife decides to go out with her friends, drinking and dancing. Her husband is fine with it, because he gets to watch sports and play on the Internet all night.

Later, her husband hears her stumble into bed around 4AM and giggles, knowing she is going to have a monster hangover.

He wakes up next morning and goes outside to the family Volvo, which she used last night.

He sighs in relief because it's all in one piece and he circles the car looking for dents and finds none.

But, wait a minute. . .

Horsing Around

A guy was sitting quietly reading his paper when his wife walked up behind him and whacked him on the head with a magazine.

"What was that for?" he asked.

"That was for the piece of paper in your pants pocket with the name Laura Lou written on it," she replied.

He explained to her, "Two weeks ago when I went to the races, Laura Lou was the name of one of the horses I bet on."

"Oh honey, I'm sorry," she said. "I should have known there was a good explanation.

Three days later he was watching a ballgame on TV when she walked up and hit him in the head again, this time with an iron skillet, which knocked him out cold.

When he came to, he asked, "What was that for?"

She replied, "Your horse just called."

Signs Your Husband May Not Love You

He brings his girlfriend to the family reunion.

He says he wants everything put in his name, but you.

He cancels his life insurance and doubles yours.

Every time you ask for sex, he says, "Let me sleep on it."

He buys you cruise tickets for your anniversary, then says, "Have a nice trip."

While driving through town together, you notice that all the hookers wave at him.

He suggests a threesome with his new friend Jill.

You find lipstick on his underwear.

The neighbor's kids look more like him everyday.

You find a knife, a pair of gloves, and a receipt for membership in the O. J. Simpson fan club in his dresser drawer

Old Friends

Charlie was visiting an old friend and his wife for dinner. When the time came to leave, his car wouldn't start, and it was too late to call the local service station.

The husband urged Charlie to stay over. There was no spare bed in the house and there wasn't even a sofa, so Charlie would have to sleep with the husband and wife.

No sooner had the husband fallen asleep when the wife tapped Charlie on the shoulder and motioned for him to come over to her.

"I couldn't do that," he whispered. "Your husband is my best friend."

"Listen Charlie," she whispered back, there isn't anything in the whole world that would wake him up now."

"I can't believe that," Charlie said. "Certainly if I get on top of you and screw you, he will wake up, won't he?"

"He certainly will not. If you don't believe me, pluck a hair out of his ass and see if that wakes him."

Charlie reached over and did it. He was amazed when the husband remained asleep. He moved over to her side of the bed and did her.

When he finished, he climbed back to his own side. It wasn't long before she tapped him on the shoulder and beckoned him again.

Again he pulled a hair to determine if his friend was asleep. This went on four times during the night. Each time Charlie screwed the woman, he first pulled out one of the husband's butt hairs.

The fifth time he pulled a hair, the husband woke up and muttered, "Listen, Charlie, I don't mind you screwing my wife, but please stop using my ass to keep score."

Free Sex

There was a gas station down south trying to increase its sales so the owner put up a sign that said, "Free Sex with every fill-up."

A redneck customer named Bubba pulled in, filled his tank, and then asked for his free sex.

The owner told Bubba to pick a number from one to ten, and if he guessed correctly, he would get his free sex. Bubba guessed nine.

The proprietor said, "No, you were close, but the number was eight. Sorry, no free sex this time."

A week later, Bubba and his buddy pulled in for another fill-up, and again he asked for his free sex.

The proprietor gave him the same story and asked him to guess the correct number.

Bubba guessed eight this time. The proprietor said, "Sorry, the correct number was seven. You were close, but no free sex this time."

As they were driving away, the friend said to Bubba, "Bubba, I think that game is rigged and he never gives away free sex."

Bubba replied, "Heck No, it ain't rigged. My wife won twice last week, and she didn't even get a fill-up."

Prostitute Fees

A young man and his date were parked on a back road a few miles from town, doing what young men and women do on back roads a few miles from town.

Things were going along well and getting pretty hot when the girl stopped the young man.

"I should have mentioned this earlier, but I'm actually a prostitute and I charge twenty dollars for sex."

The young man looked her over for a couple of seconds and then reluctantly paid her, and they got down to doing what they really came to do.

Later, the young man was smoking a cigarette as he sat in the driver's seat looking out the window.

The prostitute tapped him on the shoulder and asked, "Why aren't we going anywhere?"

"I should have mentioned this earlier, but I'm actually a taxi driver, and the fare back to town is twenty five dollars."

Sneaking Home Late

Ole staggered home very late after another evening with his drinking buddy, Sven.

He took off his shoes to avoid waking his wife, Lena. He tiptoed quietly toward the stairs leading to their upstairs bedroom, but misjudged the bottom step. As he caught himself by grabbing the banister, his body swung around and he landed heavily on the floor, on his butt.

A whiskey bottle in each back pocket broke and made the landing especially painful.

Ole sprung up, pulled down his pants, and looked in the hall mirror to see that both of his butt cheeks were cut and bleeding.

He managed to quietly find a full box of Band-Aids and began putting a Band-Aid as best he could on each place he saw blood. He then hid the now almost empty box and shuffled and stumbled his way to bed.

In the morning, Ole woke up with searing pains in both his head and butt. Lena was staring at him from across the room.

She said, "You were drunk again last night weren't you Ole?"

Ole said, "Why would you say such a mean thing to me?"

"It could be the open front door. It could be the broken glass at the bottom of the stairs. It could be the drops of blood trailing through the house, or it could be your bloodshot eyes, but mostly it's all those Band-Aids stuck on the downstairs mirror."

Hit Man

Two old friends were just about to tee off at the first hole of their local golf course when a guy carrying a golf bag called out to them, "Do you mind if I join you? My partner didn't turn up."

"Sure," they said, "You are welcome to join us."

So they started playing and enjoyed the game and the company of the newcomer.

Part way around the course, one of the friends asked the newcomer, "What do you do for a living?"

"I'm a hit man," was the reply.

"You are surely joking." was the response.

"No, I am not," he said. He reached into his golf bag, and pulled out a beautiful polished sniper's rifle with a large telescopic sight. "This is one of my tools."

"That is a beautiful telescopic sight," said the other friend, "Can I take a look through it? I think I might be able to see my house from here." So he picked up the rifle and looked through the sight in the direction of his house.

"Yeah, I can see my house. This sight is fantastic. I can see right in the window. Wow, I can see my wife in the bedroom. Ha Ha, I can see she is naked. Wait a minute, that's my neighbor in there with her. . . He's naked, too."

He turned to the hit man, "How much do you charge for a hit?"

"I'll do a flat rate, for you, one thousand dollars every time I pull the trigger"

"Can you do two for me now?"

"Sure, what do you want?"

244

"First, shoot my wife; she is always been mouthy, so shoot her in the mouth.

Then the neighbor, he used to be a friend of mine. Shoot his pecker and nuts off to teach him a lesson."

The hit man picked up the rifle and took aim, standing perfectly still for a few minutes.

"Are you going to do it or not?" said the friend impatiently.

"Just be patient," said the hit man calmly, "I think I can save you a thousand bucks."

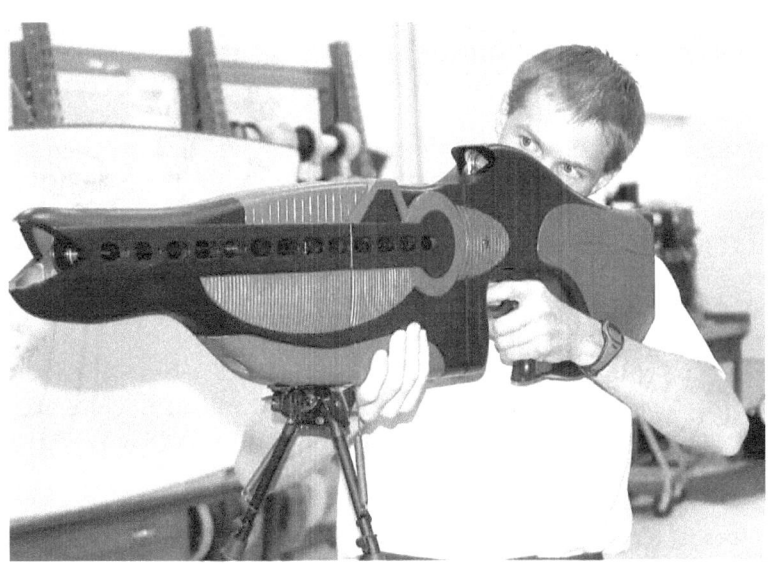

Social Disease

A gentleman permitted himself one minor indiscretion and found that after a few days he had contracted a devastating social disease.

He immediately went to the doctor.

The doctor advised him to have his pecker amputated to avoid the risk of spreading infection to other vital organs. The cost would be about two thousand dollars.

This terribly upset the man, who felt there must be a better way to take care of his problem.

He went to another physician for a second opinion and was again told that it must be cut off for his good health. The cost would be about three thousand dollars.

After discussing the matter with an associate, he discovered that there was a Chinese doctor that might be able to help and that his charges would certainly be lower than what the other doctors wanted to charge him.

He went to see the Chinese physician and the doctor gave him a thorough checkup.

The Chinese physician told him, "These American doctors are just out to take your money. If you wait for a few weeks, your pecker will fall off by itself."

Talcum Powder

A man's wife asks him to go to the store to buy some cigarettes for her, so he walks down to the store, but it was closed.

He walks a bit farther and goes into a nearby bar to use the vending machine. He glances up he sees a beautiful woman sitting at the bar and starts talking to her.

They have a couple of beers and one thing leads to another, so they go to her apartment.

After they have had their fun, he realizes that it is now three in the morning. He gets up and says, "Oh no, it is so late, my wife is going to kill me. Do you have any talcum powder?"

She gives him some talcum powder and he proceeds to rub it on his hands and then proceeds home.

His wife is waiting for him in the doorway and is very upset with him. "Where the hell have you been?"

"Well, honey, it's like this. I went to the store like you asked, but it was closed, so I went to the bar to use the vending machine. I saw this great looking woman there and we had a few drinks and one thing led to another and I ended up in bed with her."

"That's a crock, let me see your hands."

She sees his hands are covered with powder and says, "You liar. I know you went bowling again."

Email Plans

A businessman sends an email to his wife.

My dear wife,

You will surely understand that I have certain needs that you, with your fifty four years, can no longer supply. I am very happy with you and value you as a good wife.

Therefore after reading this email, I hope that you will not wrongly interpret the fact that I will be spending the evening with my twenty year old secretary at the hotel. Please do not be disturbed, I will be back home before midnight.

When the man came home, he found the following letter on the dining room table.

My dear husband,

I received your email, and thank you for your honesty. I would like to take this opportunity to remind you that you are also fifty four years old.

Also, I would like to inform you that while you read this, I will be at the Hotel Fiesta with Max, my tennis coach. He is also twenty years old, just like your secretary.

As a successful businessman and with your excellent knowledge of math, you will understand that we are in the same situation, although there is one small difference.

Twenty goes into fifty four more times than fifty four goes into twenty. Therefore, I will not be back before lunchtime tomorrow.

Nooner

A guy walks into a drinking establishment, sits at the bar, and orders a shot of whiskey. The bartender gives it to him and the man slams it down without hesitation.

The bartender watches him and the guy quickly orders another. The bartender gives him another and the guy slams it down just as fast as the first one.

The bartender asks him if everything is OK.

The guy responds, "The day started out great. I work across the street at the bank. I closed a huge deal today and thought it would be a good idea to go home for lunch, surprise my wife, and maybe get a nooner. I arrived at the house, went into the bedroom, and caught my wife in bed screwing my best friend."

The bartender pours the guy another drink and says, "Man, that sucks. Here is one on the house."

Again, the guy sucks the drink down.

The bartender asks, "So what did you say to your wife?"

The guy replies, "I looked her right in the eye, shook my finger in her face, and said, bitch, pack your stuff and get the hell out of my house."

The bartender slaps the guy on the back and pours him another, saying, "You da man. Way to tell that woman off."

The guy takes the drink and the bartender asks, "So, what did you do about your best friend? What did you say to him?"

The guy looks at the bartender and says, "I looked him right in the eye, shook my finger in his face, and said, bad doggie."

Lotto Surprise

One day, the wife comes home with a spectacular diamond ring.

"Where did you get that ring?" her husband asks.

She replies, "My boss and I played the lotto and we won, so I bought it with my share of the winnings."

A week later, his wife comes home with a long shiny fur coat.

"Where did you get that coat?" her husband asks.

She replies, "My boss and I played the lotto and we won again, so I bought it with my share of the winnings."

Another week later, his wife comes home, driving a red Ferrari.

"Where did you get that car?" her husband asks.

Again she repeats the same story about winning the lotto and spending her share of the winnings.

That evening, his wife asks him to draw her nice warm bath while she gets undressed. When she enters the bathroom, she finds that there is barely enough water in the bath to cover the plug.

"What's this?" she asks her husband.

He replies, "We sure don't want to get your lotto ticket wet, do we?"

No More Adultery

There was an old priest who was depressed because of all the people in his parish who were confessing to adultery.

The next Sunday in the pulpit he said, "If I hear one more person confess to adultery, I will immediately quit."

Everyone really liked him, so they came up with a code word. Someone who had committed adultery would say they 'had fallen'. This seemed to satisfy the old priest and things went well, until the priest died.

About a week after the new priest arrived, he visited the Mayor of the town and appeared very concerned.

The priest said, "You have to do something about the sidewalks in town. When people come into the confessional, they keep talking about having 'fallen'."

The Mayor started to laugh, realizing that no one had told the new priest about the code word.

Before the Mayor could explain, the priest shook an accusing finger at the Mayor and said, "I don't know what you are laughing about. Your wife told me that she fell three times this week."

Delivering Mail

A fellow is browsing in a pet shop and sees a parrot sitting on a little perch. It doesn't have any feet or legs. The guy says aloud, "I wonder what happened to this parrot?"

The parrot said, "I was born this way. I'm a defective parrot."

The guy replied, "You actually understood and answered me?"

"I understood every word," said the parrot. "I happen to be a highly intelligent and thoroughly educated bird."

The guy asked, "How do you hang onto your perch without any feet?"

"This is embarrassing, but since you asked, I wrap my thingy around this wooden bar like a little hook. You can't see it because of my feathers. I also speak Spanish and English, and I can converse with reasonable competence on almost any topic. My specialties are politics, religion, sports, and more. I am especially good at ornithology. You really ought to buy me. I could be a great companion."

The guy looked at the five hundred dollar price tag and said, "Sorry, but I just can't afford to pay that much money."

The parrot said, "The truth is that nobody wants me cause I don't have any feet. You can probably get me for fifty bucks. Just make the store owner an offer."

The guy offered fifty dollars, the owner took it, and he walked out with the parrot.

Weeks passed and the parrot was sensational. He had a great sense of humor, was interesting, and a great pal. He understood everything. He sympathized, and proved to be insightful. The guy was totally delighted.

One day the guy came home from work and the parrot said, "Psst," and motioned him over with one wing. "I don't know if I should tell you this or not, but it's about your wife and the postman."

"What are you talking about?" asked the guy.

"When the postman delivered the mail today, your wife greeted him at the door in a sheer nightie and kissed him passionately."

"What happened after that?"

"The postman came into the house, lifted up her nightie and began petting her all over," reported the parrot.

"Oh no, then what?"

"Then he got down on his knees and began to kiss her all over, starting with her breasts and slowly going down."

The guy asked, "Then what happened?"

"Damned if I know. I got a hard-on and fell off my perch."

Brothels

A dedicated Teamsters Union worker was attending a convention in Las Vegas and decided to check out the local brothels.

When he arrived at the first one, he asked the Madam, "Is this a union house?"

"No," she replied, "This is not a union house."

"If I pay you a hundred dollars, what cut will the girls get?"

"The house receives eighty percent and the girls receive twenty percent," she answered.

The union man was very offended at the unfair management split and stomped off down the street in search of a more equitable and unionized shop.

His search continued until finally he reached a brothel where the madam responded, "Yes sir, this is a union house. We observe all union rules.

The man asked her, "If I pay you a hundred dollars, what cut do the girls get?"

"The girls receive eighty percent and the house twenty percent."

"That's more like it." He handed the madam a hundred dollars, then looked around the room and pointed to an attractive blonde.

"I would like to go to bed with her," he said.

I am sure you would sir, but we abide by union rules in this house," said the madam.

She gestured toward a seventy-five year old woman sitting in the corner. She continued, "You must take Ethel. She has forty seven years seniority, and she is next."

Doing His Business

A man walked into a cafe, went up to the bar, and ordered a beer from the bartender.

"Certainly sir. That will be one cent."

"One cent?" the man exclaimed. "That's great."

He glanced at the menu and asked, "How much for a nice big juicy steak and a bottle of wine?"

"A nickel," the barman replied.

"A nickel?" exclaimed the man. "Where is the guy who owns this place?"

The bartender replied, "Upstairs, with my wife."

The man asked, "What is he doing upstairs with your wife?"

The bartender replied, "The same thing I am doing to his business down here."

Playing Games

Two couples were playing cards one evening. John accidentally dropped some cards on the floor.

When he bent down under the table to pick them up, he noticed that Bill's wife, Sue had her legs spread wide and wasn't wearing any underwear. John was shocked and upon trying to sit back up again, hit his head on the table and emerged red-faced.

Later, John went to the kitchen to get some refreshments.

Sue followed him and asked, "Did you see anything that you liked under there?"

Surprised by her boldness, John admitted that he did.

She said, "Well, you can have it, but it will cost you five hundred dollars."

After taking a minute or two to assess the financial as well as the moral costs of this offer, John says that he was indeed interested.

She said that since her husband Bill, works Friday afternoons and John doesn't, that John should be at her house around two on Friday afternoon.

When Friday rolled around, John showed up at Bill's house for the planned time with Sue at two pm. After paying her the agreed five hundred dollars, they went to the bedroom and conducted their sexual transaction as Sue had promised.

Afterwards, John quickly dressed and left. As usual, Bill came home from work and upon entering the house, asked his wife, "Did John come to our house this afternoon?"

Bill's wife was concerned, but answered, "Why yes, he did stop by for a few minutes this afternoon."

Her heart nearly skipped a beat when her husband asked, "And did he give you five hundred dollars?"

She assumed that somehow he had found out, and after mustering up her best poker face, she replied, "Yes, in fact he did give me five hundred dollars."

Bill, was satisfied with her answer and surprised his wife by saying, "Good, I was hoping he did. John came by the office this morning and borrowed five hundred dollars from me. He promised me he would stop by our house this afternoon on his way home and pay me back."

Costumes

A couple was invited to a masked Halloween Party, but the wife developed a headache and told her husband to go to the party alone.

He protested, but she said she was going to take an aspirin and go to bed. She told him there was no need to spoil his good time, so he took his costume and went to the party without her.

She slept for about an hour and woke up and her headache was completely gone, so she decided to go the party. She knew her husband did not know her costume, so she thought she would have some fun by watching him to see how he acted without her.

She joined the party and soon spotted her husband cavorting around on the dance floor, dancing with every nice girl he could. She sidled up to him seductively, and convinced him to leave his partner. She let him go as far as he wished.

Finally, he whispered a little proposition in her ear and she agreed, so they went to one of the cars and had a little fling.

Just before unmasking at midnight, she slipped away, went home, put the costume away, and jumped into bed. She wondered what kind of explanation he would have for his behavior.

She was sitting there reading when he came in and asked him what kind of a time he had.

He said, "Oh, the same old thing. You know I never have a good time when you're not there."

Then she asked, "Did you dance much?"

He replied, "I never even danced one dance. When I arrived, I met Carl, Tom, and some other guys, so we went into the den and played poker all evening."

He continued, "You are not going to believe what happened to the guy I loaned my costume to."

Divorce

Dividing Assets

A man was reading the paper when an ad caught his eye.

"Porsche, $500, New"

The man thought that it was very unusual to sell a Porsche for five hundred dollars, and thought it might be a joke.

He also thought it was worth a try, so he went to the address listed in the ad. Sure enough, a lady answered the door and confirmed that she had an almost brand new Porsche for sale.

She sold him that the ad was correct and she would sell it to him for five hundred dollars.

"Wow!" the man said. "Can I take it for a test drive?"

The man found that the car ran perfectly and raced it back to the lady's house.

"Why are you willing to sell this great Porsche for only five hundred dollars?"

She said, "My husband just ran off with his young and beautiful secretary, and he told me I could have the house and the furniture as long as I sold his Porsche and sent him the money."

Lawyer Questions

A Polish guy married a Canadian girl after he had been in Canada for a while.

His English was far from perfect, but they got on very well, until one fateful day.

He went into a lawyer's office and asked the lawyer if he could arrange a divorce for him, immediately

The lawyer said that he could, but the speed of getting a divorce would depend on the circumstances and asked him the following questions:

Lawyer: Have you any grounds?
Pole: Ja, Ja, an acre and half.

Lawyer: Does your wife beat you up?
Pole: No, I'm always up before her.

Lawyer: Is your wife a nagger?
Pole: No, she white.

Lawyer: Why do you want this divorce?
Pole: She going to kill me.

Lawyer: What makes you think that?
Pole: I got proof.

Lawyer: What kind of proof?
Pole: She bought a bottle at the drug store, and put it on the shelf in the bathroom.

Lawyer: What kind of bottle?
Pole: The label says, Polish Remover.

Weekend Racket

A consultant was in court testifying in regard to the divorce proceedings against his wife.

The attorney asked, "Tell us about the incident that first caused you to entertain suspicions as to your wife's infidelity."

The man replied that he traveled all week and so naturally when he came home, he was especially attentive to his wife.

He continued by telling how one weekend they had been engaged in the midst of some very heavy lovemaking when the old lady in the apartment next door pounded on the wall.

She yelled, "Can't you stop all that lovemaking racket at least on the weekends?"

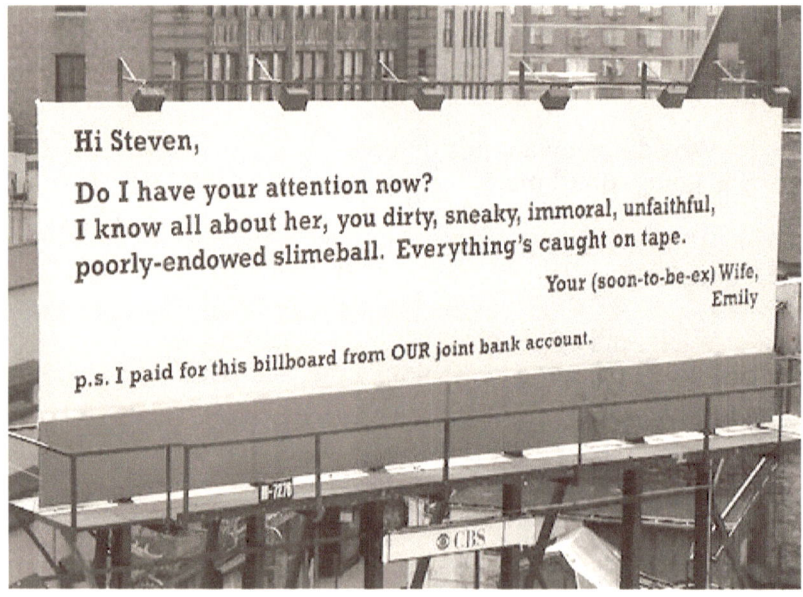

The Ad

A woman gets married for the first time, but soon gets divorced, because her husband beat her constantly.

She gets married again, but gets divorced again, because her husband ran away.

Following the advice of a friend, she puts an ad in the local paper simply saying, "I am looking for a man who won't run away, and won't beat me, but will give me great sex."

A week later the door bell rings and the woman gets up to answer it.

She opens the door and sees a man with no arms and no legs sitting comfortably in a wheel chair.

The woman asks him, "What is it that you want?"

"I have come in regard to the ad you put in the paper," he says.

"But you have no legs or arms," she replies.

"That should prove to you that I will not run away or hit you," he calmly answers.

"What makes you think you can give me great sex," she asks?

"How do you think I rang the door bell," he replies.

A Little Company

An attractive woman entered a pet shop. When the clerk offered assistance, she explained that she was recently divorced, and was looking for a small dog for company.

The clerk explained that the name of the store was 'Exotic Pets' and that unfortunately, they did not stock cats, dogs, fish or any commonplace pets. He did say, however, that he had something which might be ideal. He took the woman into a back room, walked over to a terrarium, and pointed proudly to a large bullfrog which sat inside it. "Would that suit your needs?" he asked.

The woman answered, that she hardly thought an amphibian would be a suitable companion.

"Ah," replied the salesman, "This amphibian has been carefully trained to perform oral sex upon women."

At this the woman's eyes lit up. She eagerly negotiated a price of five hundred dollars for the frog, and left with it in her expectant possession.

Arriving home, she drew a bubble bath, poured a glass of champagne, and relaxed in anticipation. When she was thoroughly mellow, she dried herself, and arranged herself nude on her bed. Parting her thighs, she placed the frog between them, closed her eyes, and waited.

Nothing happened.

She prodded the frog. Still nothing.

She moved it up further toward her body. Nothing.

She ordered it to perform. No response.

After an hour of this frustration, she grabbed her phone, and called the pet shop.

When the clerk answered, she complained loudly that she had been cheated. The clerk apologized profusely, wrote down her address, and told her he would be right over.

Ten minutes later, he knocked on the door, and the woman answered, wearing a nightgown. He asked her to demonstrate the problem.

She obliged, by disrobing and assuming her former position, with the frog in place. The frog made no movement.

"Do you see?" she asked.

"Yes, I do," said the man. Then, addressing the frog as he removed his necktie and shirt he said, "Now, I'm only going to show you this one more time. . ."

Swearing Off Women

Chuck and Larry had just become divorced and swore they would never have anything to do with women again. They were best friends and they decided to move up to Alaska so they would never have to look at a woman again.

They arrived in Alaska and went into a trader's store and told him, "Give us enough supplies to last two men for one year."

The trader collected the supplies and gear together and on top of each one's supplies he laid a board with a hole in it with fur around the hole.

The guys asked, "What's that board for?"

The trader said, "Where you're going there are no women and you might need this."

They said, "No way. We have sworn off women for life."

The trader said, "Take the boards with you, and if you don't use them I will refund your money next year.

The next year the Chuck came into the trader's store and said, "Give me enough supplies to last one man for one year."

The trader asked, "Weren't you in here last year with a partner?"

"Yeah," replied Chuck.

"Where is he?" asked the trader.

"I shot him," he said.

"Why?"

"I caught him in bed with my board."

Grounds for Divorce

A judge was interviewing a woman regarding her pending divorce, and asked, "What are the grounds for your divorce?"

She replied, "About four acres and a nice little home in the middle of the property with a stream running by."

"No," he said, "I mean what is the foundation of this case?"

"It is made of concrete, brick, and mortar," She responded.

"I mean," he continued, "What are your relations like?"

"I have an aunt and uncle living here in town, and also my husband's parents."

He said, "Do you have a real grudge?"

"No, we have a two-car carport and have never really needed a garage."

"Is there any infidelity in your marriage?"

"Yes, both my son and daughter have stereo sets. We don't necessarily like the music, but the answer to your questions is yes."

"Madam, does your husband ever beat you up?"

"Yes, about twice a week he gets up earlier than I do."

Finally, in frustration, the judge asked, "Lady, why do you want a divorce?"

"Oh, I don't want a divorce," She replied. "I have never wanted a divorce. My husband does. I don't know why, but he said he can't communicate with me."

Divorce Alternative

Dick and Jane, a married couple, are driving along a highway doing sixty mph with the husband behind the wheel.

Jane suddenly looks over at Dick and says, "Honey, I know we have been married for twenty years, but I want a divorce."

Dick says nothing, but slowly increases the speed to seventy.

Jane then says, "I don't want you to try to talk me out of it, because I have been having an affair with your best friend David, and he is a better lover than you are."

Again Dick stays quiet but speeds up as his anger increases.

"I want the house, too," she insists.

Again the husband speeds up, to eighty.

She says, "I want the car, too."

He just drives faster and faster and by now he's up to ninety.

Jane continues, "I want the bank accounts, and all the credit cards, too."

Dick slowly starts to veer toward a bridge overpass piling. This makes her a bit nervous, so she says, "Isn't there anything you want?"

Dick says, "No, I have everything I need."

She says, "What do you have?"

Just before they slam into the wall at a hundred miles an hour, he smiles and says, "The airbag."

Divorce Tidbits

When a man steals your wife, there is no better revenge than to let him keep her.

A man appears before a judge one day, asking for a divorce. The judge quietly reviews some papers and then says, "Please tell me why you are seeking a divorce."

"Because," the man says, "I live in a two-story house."

The judge replies, "What kind of a reason is that? What is the big deal about a two-story house?"

The man answers, "Well judge, one story is, 'I have a headache' and the other story is, 'It's that time of the month'."

It had promised to be a sensational divorce case, with the wife accused of incredible escapades. Testifying before her own attorney, she projected an image of sweet innocence, told a tale of wifely fidelity and sacrifice, and was quite believable.

When it was time for cross-examination though, the husband's lawyer arose and said, "Isn't it true that on the night of June 12, in a driving rainstorm, you had sexual intercourse with a certain circus midget on the handle bars of a careening motorcycle as it raced across a private golf course reaching speeds in excess of seventy-five miles per hour?"

She turned pale, but retained her remarkable self-control and composure.

Her voice was almost serene in its innocence as she asked, "What was that date again?"

269

A man and woman are having marriage problems, and decide to end it after a very short time together. After a most brief attempt to reconcile, the couple goes to court to finalize their break-up.

The judge asks the husband, "What has brought you to the point where you are not able to keep this marriage together?"

The husband says, "In the six weeks we have been together, we haven't been able to agree on one thing.

The wife says, "Seven weeks."

A husband is desperate to end an argument and offers to buy his wife a new car. She curtly declines his offer by saying, "That is not quite what I had in mind."

Frantically he offers her a new house.

Again she rejects his offer, "That is not quite what I had in mind."

He asks, "What did you have in mind?"

She retorts, "I would like a divorce."

He answers, "I had not planned on spending quite that much."

Ageing

Thoughts About Ageing

Maturity for some brings the inevitability of dalliances and divorce.

For others, it brings the folly of facelifts, and fun of flatulence.

Time endears but cannot fade,
the memories that love has made.

Statistics show that at the age of seventy there are five women for every man. What an ironic time for a guy to get that kind of odds.

Age is a relative thing - Consider dead fish and good wine.

The best contraceptive for old people is nudity.

You know you are getting old when you reach the age where happy hour means a nap.

Eighty-year-old LuAnn bursts into the TV room of the retirement home with her fist clenched above her head. "The first person that can guess what is in my hand can have sex with me tonight," she announces to the room.

An old man looks up from the pool table and says, "An elephant."

LuAnn thinks about it for a second and says, "Close enough."

The greatest weakness of most humans is their hesitancy to tell others how much they love them while they are still alive.

Old is when your friends compliment you on your new alligator shoes and you are barefoot.

Those who love deeply never grow old; they may die of old age, but they die young.

Old is when the porn you bring home is, "Debby Does Dialysis."

Male menopause is more fun than female menopause. Females gain weight and get hot flashes. Males date young girls and drive hot motorcycles.

A ninety year old woman returns from a date with a ninety year old man. Her roommate asks how it went.

She replies, "I had to slap his face three times."

Her roommate says, "That's terrible, was he getting fresh with you?"

She says, "No, I had to make sure he wasn't dead."

Old is when your doctor doesn't give you x-rays anymore, just holds you up to the light.

Old is when a sexy babe catches your fancy and your pacemaker opens the nearest garage door.

A foursome of elderly gentlemen came back after a round of golf. At the 19th hole in the Clubhouse, the pro asked them, "How did your game go?"

The first said he had a good round with 25 riders. The second said he did OK with 16 riders. The third said not too bad since he had 10 riders. The fourth was disappointed and said that he played badly with only two riders.

The pro was confounded by this term 'rider', but not wanting to show his ignorance just smiled and wish them better golf the next time. He then approached Jerry the bartender and asked, "Jerry, can you tell me what does this term 'riders' mean?"

Jerry smiled and explained that a 'rider' is when you have hit a shot long enough to take a ride on a golf cart.

If plastic surgeons get any more proficient, they will put the undertakers out of business, because people who are dying, never looked better.

During their silver anniversary, a wife said to husband, "Do you remember when you proposed to me, I was so overwhelmed that I didn't talk for an hour?"

The hubby replied, "Yes dear, that was the happiest hour of my life."

My 80 year old father and I saw an attractive woman wearing an evening gown with leg openings going all the way up to her waist.

"Why do they wear gowns like that?" he asked.

"Maybe that style makes their legs look longer," I speculated.

"No," he said, "I think it makes the men look longer."

Henry and Doris were sitting in the lounge of the old folks' home one evening and Henry is wearing his pajamas.

Doris whispered, "Henry, fix your pajamas, your willy is sticking out."

Henry looked down, and said, "Don't flatter yourself, dear. My willy is just hanging out."

An old man in his eighty's got up and was putting on his coat.

His wife said, "Where are you going?"

He said, "I am going to the doctor."

She said, "Why? Are you sick?"

"No," he said. "I am going to get me some of those Viagra pills."

So his wife got up out of her rocker and was putting on her sweater and he said, "Where are you going?"

She said, "I'm going to the doctor too."

He said, "Why?"

She said, "If you are going to start using that rusty old thing again, I'm going to get a tetanus shot."

Flatulence

Flatulence is a pleasant thing,
It gives the belly ease,
It warms the bed in winter,
And suffocates the fleas.

A fart can be quiet,
A fart can be loud,
Some leave a powerful,
Poisonous cloud.

A fart can be short,
Or a fart can be long,
Some farts have been known
To sound like a song.

A fart can create
A most curious medley,
A fart can be harmless,
Or silent, and deadly.

A fart might not smell,
While others are vile,
A fart may pass quickly
Or linger a while.

A fart can occur
In a number of places
And leave everyone there
With strange looks on their faces.

From wide-open prairie
To a small elevator,
A fart will find all of
Us sooner or later.

But farts are all bad
Is simply not true.
We must never forget
Sweet old farts like you.

A Facelift

A woman in her forties went to a plastic surgeon for a face-lift. The doctor told her of a new procedure called, "The Knob."

A small knob is planted on the back of woman's head, and it can be turned to tighten up the skin to produce the effect of a brand new facelift whenever the previous one starts to sag. The woman chose to get the procedure.

Fifteen years later, she went back to the surgeon. "All these years everything has been working just fine," the woman began, "I've had to turn the knob on a number of occasions and I have always loved the results."

"I'm glad it has been so successful for you," he replies.

"Recently, I have developed two annoying problems. First of all, I have these terrible bags developing under my eyes, and the knob won't get rid of them."

The doctor looked at her closely and said, "Those aren't bags. Those are your breasts."

"Well," she replied, "I guess that explains the goatee."

More Flatulence

There was an old married couple that had lived happily together for nearly fifty years. The only friction in their marriage was caused by the husband's terrible flatulence every morning as he awoke. The noise would always wake up his wife and the smell would cause her eyes to water as she choked and gasped for air.

Every morning he told her that he couldn't help it. She begged him to see a doctor to see if anything could be done, but the husband would not hear of it. He told her that it was just a natural bodily function and laughed as she waved the fumes away with her hands.

Every day she told him that there was nothing natural about it and if he didn't stop, he would fart out his guts one day.

The years went by and the wife continued to suffer and the husband continued to ignore her warnings about farting his guts out. One Thanksgiving morning, before dawn, she began to prepare the family feast of pumpkin pie, mashed potatoes, gravy, and turkey.

While she was taking out the turkey's innards, a thought occurred to her about how she might solve her problem. She placed the turkey guts into a bowl. While he was still asleep, she pulled back the covers and gently pulled back her husband's jockey shorts. She then placed all the turkey guts into her husband's underwear, pulled them up, replaced the covers, and tiptoed down to finish preparing the family meal.

Several hours later, she heard her husband awake with his normal loud butt-trumpet, soon followed by a blood curdling scream and the sound of frantic footsteps as her husband ran to the bathroom.

The wife could not control herself and her eyes began to tear up as she rolled on the floor laughing. She finally got even.

About twenty minutes later, her husband came downstairs in his blood stained shorts with a look of horror in his eyes. She bit her lip to keep from laughing and she asked him what was wrong.

He said, "Honey, you were right. All those years you warned me about my flatulence and I didn't listen to you."

"What do you mean?" asked his wife.

"You always told me that I would end up farting my guts out one day and it finally happened, but with God's help and these two fingers, I think I got them all back in."

Someone Has Soiled the Air!

SOME SUGGESTIONS:

—Say, "Oh, mercy! I can't breathe!"
Ever so casually, open a window or two.
—Say nothing, and hold your breath.
Cover nose and mouth with scented handkerchief until the scourge dissipates
Whip out your hand fan
Pray silently.

279

Fifty Dollars

Jimmy and his wife Aggie went to the state fair every year and every year, he would say, "Aggie, I would like to ride in that helicopter."

Aggie always replied, "I know Jimmy, but that helicopter ride is fifty dollars and fifty dollars is fifty dollars."

One year, they went to the fair and Jimmy said, "Aggie, I am almost sixty years old, if I don't ride that helicopter now, I might never get another chance."

She replied, "That helicopter ride is fifty dollars and fifty dollars is fifty dollars."

The pilot overheard the couple bickering and said, "Folks, I'll make you a deal. I will take the both of you up for a ride. If you can stay quiet for the entire ride and not say a word, I won't charge you, but if you say one word, it's fifty dollars."

Jimmy and Aggie agreed, and up they went for a ride.

The pilot did all kinds of fancy maneuvers, but not a word was spoken. He did his daredevil tricks over and over again, but still not a word.

When they landed, the pilot turned to Jimmy and said, "By golly, I did everything I could to get you to yell out, but you didn't. I am really impressed."

Jimmy replied, "I was going to say something when Aggie fell out, but fifty dollars is fifty dollars."

Life at 60+

Q: Where can women over the age of 60 find young, sexy men, who are interested in them?
A: Try a bookstore under fiction.

Q: What can a man do while his wife is going through menopause?
A: Keep busy. If you are handy with tools, you can finish the basement. When you are done you will have a place to live.

Q: How can you increase the heart rate of your 60+ year old husband?
A: Tell him you are pregnant.

Q: How can you avoid spotting a wrinkle every time you walk by a mirror?
A: Take off your glasses.

Q: Why should 60+ year old people use valet parking?
A: Valets don't forget where they park your car.

Q: Is it common for 60+ year olds to have problems with short term memory storage?
A: Storing memory is not a problem, retrieving it is a problem.

Q: What is the most common remark made by 60+ year olds when they enter antique stores?
A: "I remember these."

One Last Fling

An elderly spinster called the lawyer's office and told the receptionist she wanted to see the lawyer about having a will prepared. The receptionist suggested they set up an appointment for a convenient time for her to come into the office.

The woman replied, "I have lived alone all my life, I rarely see anyone, and I don't like to go out. Would it be possible for the lawyer to come to my house?"

The receptionist checked with the attorney who agreed and he went to the woman's home for the meeting to discuss her estate and the will.

The lawyer's first question was, "Would you please tell me what you have in assets and how you would like them to be distributed under the terms of your will?"

She replied, "Besides the furniture and accessories you see, I have fifty thousand dollars in my savings account at the bank."

"Tell me, how would you like the fifty grand to be distributed?" the lawyer asked.

The spinster said, "I have lived a reclusive life, people hardly ever notice me, so I would like them to notice when I pass on. I would like to provide forty-five thousand for my funeral."

The lawyer remarked, "For forty-five thousand you will be able to have a funeral that will certainly be noticed and will leave a lasting impression on everyone, but tell me, what would you like to do with the remaining five thousand?"

The old woman replied, "Since I never married, and have lived alone almost my entire life, and have never slept with a man, I would like you to use the five thousand dollars to arrange for a man to sleep with me."

He remarked, "This is a very unusual request, but I will see what I can do to arrange it and get back to you."

That evening, the lawyer was at home telling his wife about the eccentric spinster and her weird request.

After thinking about how much she could do around the house with five thousand dollars and with a bit of coaxing, she made her husband agree to provide the service himself.

She said, "I will drive you over to her house tomorrow morning and wait in the car until you're finished."

The next morning, she drove him to the spinster's house and waited while he went into the house.

She waited for over an hour, but her husband didn't come out, so she blew the car horn.

The bedroom window opened, the lawyer stuck his head out and yelled, "Pick me up tomorrow. She's going to let the County bury her."

Hearing Problems

An old man decided his wife was getting hard of hearing. He called her doctor to make an appointment to have her hearing checked.

The doctor said he could see her in two weeks, but meanwhile there was a simple test the husband could do to give the him some idea of the severity of the problem.

"Here's what you do. Start about forty feet away from her, and speak in a normal conversational tone to find out if she hears you. If not, go to thirty feet, twenty feet, and so on until you get a response."

That evening she is in the kitchen cooking dinner, and he is in the living room, and he thinks to himself, "I'm about forty feet away, let's see what happens."

"Honey, what's for supper?" No response.

He moves to the other end of the room, about thirty feet away.

"Honey, what's for supper?" No response.

He moves into the dining room, about twenty feet away.

"Honey, what's for supper?" No response.

He now moves right next to the kitchen door, ten feet away.

"Honey, what's for supper?"

Still no response, so he walks right up behind her and says, "Honey, what's for supper?"

She turns and says, "For the fifth time, I said chicken."

Ravage Me

One day, a farmer was in town picking up supplies for his farm. He stopped by the hardware store and picked up a bucket and an anvil. Then, he stopped by the livestock dealer to buy a couple of chickens and a goose.

However, he now had a problem how to carry all of his purchases home. The livestock dealer said, "Why don't you put the anvil in the bucket, carry the bucket in one hand, put a chicken under each arm and carry the goose in your other hand."

"Hey, thanks." the farmer said, and off he went. While walking he met a little old lady who told him she was lost. She asked, "Can you tell me how to get to 1515 Morningside Lane."

The farmer said, "As a matter of fact, I live at 1616 Morningside Lane. You can follow me. Let's take my short cut and go down this alley. We will be there in no time."

The little old lady said, "I am a lonely widow without a husband to defend me. How do I know that when we get in the alley you won't hold me up against the wall, pull up my skirt, and ravish me?"

The farmer said, "Holy smokes lady. I am carrying a bucket, an anvil, two chickens, and a goose. How in the world could I possibly hold you up against the wall and do that?"

The lady said, "Set the goose down, cover him with the bucket, put the anvil on top of the bucket, and I'll hold the chickens."

Bad Hearing

A senior couple pulls into a gas station and the attendant asks how he might help.

Old Man: "Fill it up."

Old Lady: "What did he say?"

Old Man [yelling]: "He asked what we wanted and I told him to fill it up."

Attendant: "So, where are you heading?"

Old Man: "To Chicago to see our grandchildren."

Old Lady: "What did he say?"

Old Man [yelling]: "He asked where we're going and I told him to Chicago."

Attendant: "Where are you coming from?"

Old Man: "We started our trip from Pittsburgh."

Old Lady: "What did he say?"

Old Man [yelling]: "He asked where we are coming from and I said Pittsburgh."

Attendant: "I dated a girl from Pittsburgh once. She wouldn't shut up and she was lousy in bed."

Old Lady: "What did he say?"

Old Man [yelling]: "He says he knows you."

The Physical

Walt was getting on in years and decided to go to the doctor for his annual physical.

All of his tests came back with normal results. Doctor Bush said, "Walt, everything looks great physically. How are you doing mentally and emotionally? Are you at peace with yourself, and do you have a good relationship with your God?"

Walt replied, "I get along with God. He knows I have poor eyesight, so He has fixed it so that when I get up in the middle of the night to go to the bathroom the light turns on when I pee, and then the light turns off when I'm done."

"Wow," commented the doctor, "That's incredible."

A while later, Doctor Bush called Walt's wife.

"Joannie," he said, "Walt is fine. Physically he is in great shape. However, I had to call because I am curious about his relationship with God. Is it true that he gets up during the night and the light turns on in the bathroom and then the light turns off when he is finished?"

Joannie exclaimed, "That old fool. He's peeing in the refrigerator again."

Doing Grandmother

An old drunk walks into a biker bar, sits down at the bar and orders a drink. He looks around and sees three men sitting at a corner table.

He gets up, staggers to the table, leans over, looks the biggest, meanest, biker in the face and says, "I went by your grandma's house today and I saw her in the hallway buck naked. Man, she is one fine looking woman."

The biker looks at him and doesn't say a word.

His buddies are confused, because he is one bad biker and would fight at the drop of a hat.

The drunk leans on the table again and says, "I got it on with your grandma and she is good, the best I ever had."

The biker's buddies are starting to get really angry, but the biker still says nothing.

The drunk leans on the table one more time and says, "I'll tell you something else boy, your grandma liked it."

At this point the biker stands up, takes the drunk by the shoulders, looks him square in the eyes and says,

"Grandpa, go home. You're drunk."

Benefits of Being over Sixty

Kidnappers are not very interested in you.

In a hostage situation you are likely to be released first.

No one expects you to run into a burning building.

People call at 9 PM and ask, "Did I wake you?"

People no longer view you as a hypochondriac.

There is nothing left to learn the hard way.

Things you buy now, won't wear out.

You can eat dinner at 4 P.M.

You can live without sex, but not without glasses.

You enjoy hearing about other peoples operations.

You get into heated arguments about pension plans.

You have a party and the neighbors don't even realize it.

You no longer think of speed limits as a challenge.

You can sing along with elevator music.

Your investment in health insurance is beginning to pay off.

Your joints are more accurate meteorologists than the national weather service.

Your secrets are safe with your friends, because they can't remember them either.

Lunch Fun at the Home

A woman working in an old folk's home gets a bit bored with the patients not responding to anything and decides to spice things up.

The next day, just before lunch she goes around the tables.

At the first table she lifts her skirt and yells, "Super Fanny!"

The old guys start drooling.

At the second table she lifts her skirt and yells, "Super Fanny!"

The guys start taking his heart attack pills.

At the next table she lifts her skirt and says, "Super Fanny!"

There is no response from the lone old man sitting at the table. She lifts her skirt again and yells louder this time, "Super Fanny!"

Finally a reply comes from the old guy, "I think I'll have the Soup, the Fanny looks off today."

Stamina

Two guys, one seventy and one eighty, were sitting on their usual park bench one morning.

The eighty year old had just finished his morning jog and wasn't even short of breath.

The seventy year old was amazed at his friend's stamina and asked him what he did to have so much energy.

The eighty year old said, "I eat rye bread every day. It keeps my energy level high and I have developed great stamina with the ladies."

On the way home, the seventy year old stops in at the bakery.

While he was looking around, the lady in the bakery asked if he needed help.

He said, "Do you have rye bread?"

She said, "Yes, there is a whole shelf of rye bread, would you like some?"

He said, "I want five loaves."

She said, "My goodness, five loaves. It will get hard."

He replied, "Does everybody in the world know about this rye bread but me?"

Hot Down Here

There was a couple from Michigan, who decided to go to Florida for a few days to thaw out during one particularly cold winter.

They had some difficulty coordinating travel schedules, because they both worked. They discussed the matter and decided the husband would leave for Florida on a certain day and the wife would follow him the day after.

The man made it down to Florida as planned and went directly to his hotel. Once in his room, he decided to open his laptop and send an e-mail to his wife.

He accidentally missed one letter while typing his wife's e-mail address and sent the e-mail off without realizing his error.

In another part of the country a widow had just returned from the funeral of her husband, who had been a Pastor.

She decided to check her e-mail because she was expecting to hear from her husband's relatives and friends. She read the first message and let out a loud scream, fainted, and fell to the floor.

The woman's son rushed into the room and found his mother lying on the floor. He glanced up at the computer screen and saw the following:

To: My Loving Wife

I have arrived. I just checked in and everything has been prepared for your arrival here tomorrow. Looking forward to seeing you then.

Your devoted husband,

P.S. Sure is hot down here.

Bus Trip

A senior citizen's group charters a bus from Cincinnati to Branson, Missouri.

As they enter Missouri, an elderly woman approaches the driver and says, "I have just been molested!"

The driver felt that she had fallen asleep and had a dream, so he tells her to go back and sit down.

A short time later, another old woman comes forward, and claims that she was also molested.

The driver thought he had a bus load of old loonies. Who would want to be molesting those old ladies?

About ten minutes later, a third old lady comes up and says that she had been molested also.

The bus driver decides that he had enough, and pulls into the first rest area. When he turns the lights on and stands up, he sees an old man on his hands and knees crawling in the aisle.

The driver says, "Hey gramps, what are you doing down there?"

"I lost my toupee. I thought I found it three times, but every time I try to grab for it, it starts moving."

Seven Dwarfs of Menopause

Itchy, Bitchy, Sweaty, Sleepy, Bloated, Forgetful & Psycho

IT'S THAT TIME
OF THE MONTH
AGAIN

Bed Games

An old married couple no sooner hits the pillow when the old man passes gas and says, "Seven points."

His wife rolls over and says, "What in the world was that?"

The old man replied, "I am playing fart football."

A few minutes later his wife lets a barker go and says, "Touchdown, tie score."

After about five minutes the old man lets another one go and says, "Aha, I'm ahead fourteen to seven."

Not to be outdone, the wife roars out another round one and says, "Touchdown. Tie score."

Five seconds go by and she lets out a little squeaker and says, "Field goal, I lead seventeen to fourteen."

Now the pressure is on the old man. He refuses to get beat by a woman, so he strains real hard. Defeat is totally unacceptable, and he gives it everything he can muster, but accidentally craps in the bed.

The wife says, "What the heck was that?"

The old man says, "Half-time, switch sides."

Advice for Husbands about Aging Wives

It is important for men to remember that as women grow older it becomes more difficult for them to maintain the same quality of housekeeping they did when they were younger. When men notice this, they should try not to yell. Let me relate how I handle the situation.

When I chucked my job and took early retirement a year ago, it became necessary for her to get a full-time job both for extra income and for health insurance benefits that we need. She was a trained lab tech when we met thirty some years ago and was fortunate to land a job at the local medical center.

It was shortly after she started working at this job that I noticed that she was beginning to show her age. I usually get home from fishing or hunting about the same time she gets home from work. Although she knows how hungry I am, she almost always says that she has to rest for half an hour or so before she starts supper. I try not to yell at her when this happens. Instead, I tell her to take her time. I understand that she is not as young as she used to be. I just tell her to wake me when she finally gets supper on the table.

She used to wash and dry the dishes as soon as we finished eating. It is now not unusual for them to sit on the table for several hours after supper. I do what I can by reminding her several times each evening that they aren't cleaning themselves.

I know she appreciates this, as it does seem to help her get them done before she goes to bed.

Our washer and dryer are in the basement. When she was younger, she used to be able to go up and down the stairs all day and not get tired. Now that she is older she seems to get tired so much more quickly. Sometimes she says she just can't make another trip down those steps. I don't make a big issue of this. As long as she finishes up the laundry the next evening I am willing to overlook it.

Not only that, but unless I need something ironed to wear to the Monday's lodge meeting or to Wednesday's or Saturday's poker club or to Tuesday's or Thursday's bowling or something like that, I will tell her to wait until the next evening to do the ironing. This gives her a little more time to do some of those odds and ends things like shampooing the dog, vacuuming, or dusting. Also, if I have had a really good day fishing, this allows her to gut and scale the fish as a more leisurely pace.

The wife is starting to complain a little occasionally. Not often, mind you, but just enough for me to notice. For example, she will say that it is difficult for her to find time to pay the monthly bills during her lunch hour. In spite of her complaining, I continue to try to offer encouragement. I tell her to stretch it out over two or even three days. That way she won't have to rush so much. I also remind her that missing lunch completely now and then wouldn't hurt her any, if you know what I mean.

When doing simple jobs she seems to think she needs more rest periods than she used to. A couple of weeks ago she said she had to take a break when she was only half finished mowing the yard.

I try to not embarrass her when she needs these little extra rest breaks. I tell her to fix herself a nice, big, cold glass of freshly squeezed lemonade and just sit for a while. I tell her that as long as she is making one for herself, she may as well make one for me to save an extra trip, and to take her break by the hammock so she can talk with me until I fall asleep.

I know that I probably look like a saint in the way I support her on a daily basis. I'm not saying that the ability to show this much consideration is easy. Many men will find it difficult. Some will find it impossible. No one knows better than I do how frustrating women can become as they get older. My purpose in writing this is simply to suggest that you make the effort.

I realize that achieving the exemplary level of showing consideration I have attained is out of reach for the average man. However guys, even if you just yell at your wife a little less often because of this article, I will consider writing it was worthwhile.

This article was found next to the author's body. The cause of death is still under investigation.

New Boots

Ted and Alice, an elderly couple, just moved to the great state of Texas.

Ted always wanted a pair of authentic cowboy boots and he spotted a pair on sale one day. He buys them and walks proudly as wears his new cowboy boots home.

He walks into the house and asks Alice, "Notice anything different about me?"

Alice looks him over and says, "Nope."

Ted storms off into the bathroom, undresses, and walks back into the room completely naked except for the new boots.

He looks at Alice and asks, "Notice anything different now?"

Alice looks up and says, "I don't know what's different? It is hanging down today. It was hanging down yesterday, and it will be hanging down tomorrow.

He is becoming very upset with her and yells, "Do you know why it is hanging down? It's hanging down because it is looking at my new boots."

Alice glances back at him and replies, "Shoulda bought a hat, Ted. Shoulda bought a hat."

Pending Nuptials

Two senior citizen gentlemen are sitting at the local park having a discussion.

The first one says to the second, "So I hear you are getting married?"

"Yep!"

"Do I know her?"

"Nope!"

"Is the woman good looking?"

"Not really."

"Is she a good cook?"

"No, she doesn't cook very well."

"Does she have a big bank account?"

"No. She is as poor as a church mouse."

"Well then, is she good in bed?"

"I don't know."

"Why in the world do you want to marry her then?"

"Because she can still drive."

Flatulence and Nudists

John is in Amsterdam and visits a nudist colony there.

While wandering around naked he spots a gorgeous blonde and he immediately gets an erection. The woman notices his erection, comes over, and says, "Sir, did you call for me?"

John replies, "No."

She says, "It's a rule here that if I give you an erection, it means you called for me."

She then lays him down and starts making love to him.

Later that day John visits the sauna, but as he sits down, he farts. A huge big hairy guy gets up, drops his towel to show a huge erection, and says, "Sir, did you call for me?"

John replies, "No."

The man says, "It's a rule that when you fart, it implies you called for me."

The man then knocks John to the floor and has his way with him.

As soon as he is finished John rushes back to his room, grabs all his things, and heads for the exit. On his way out he is stopped by the manager who asks, "Can I help you?"

John says, "Here are my room keys I am leaving early."

The manager asks why and John replies, "I am sixty years old, I get an erection once a week, but I fart twenty times a day."

Shoplifting

A ninety year old woman was arrested for shop lifting.

When she went before the judge he asked her, "What did you steal?"

She replied, "A can of peaches."

The judge asked her why she had stolen them and she replied that she was hungry.

The judge then asked her how many peaches were in the can and she replied six.

The judge then said, "I will give you six days in jail."

Before the judge could finish pronouncing the punishment the woman's husband spoke up and asked the judge if he could say something.

The judge said, "What is it you wish to say?"

The husband said, "She also stole a can of peas."

Swinging

Defense Attorney: What is your age?
Woman: I am ninety years old.

Defense Attorney: Please tell the court what happened to you?
Woman: I was sitting in my swing on my front porch, when a young man came creeping up on the porch and sat down beside me.

Defense Attorney: Did you know him?
Woman: No, but he sure was friendly.

Defense Attorney: What happened after he sat down?
Woman: He started to rub my thighs.

Defense Attorney: Did you stop him?
Woman: No, I didn't stop him.

Defense Attorney: Why not?
Woman: It felt good. Nobody had done that since my husband passed away thirty years ago.

Defense Attorney: What happened next?
Woman: He began to rub my breasts.

Defense Attorney: Did you stop him then?
Woman: No, I did not stop him.

Defense Attorney: Why not?
Woman: His rubbing made me feel all alive and excited. I haven't felt that good in years.

Defense Attorney: What happened next?
Woman: I was feeling so spicy, I just laid down and said to him 'Take me young man, take me'.

Defense Attorney: Did he take you?
Woman: No, he just yelled, 'April Fool' and that's when I shot the bastard.

Rest Homes

Mrs. Murphy and Mrs. Cohen lived next door to each other for over forty years. One day Mrs. Murphy came to Mrs. Cohen and said, "These houses are becoming too much for us, let's sell them and move into rest homes where people will take care of us."

The two old ladies each went to a home from her respective religion. It was not long before Mrs. Murphy felt lonesome for Mrs. Cohen, so one day she asked to be driven to the Jewish Home to visit her old friend.

When she arrived, she was greeted with open arms, hugs, and kisses. Mrs. Murphy said, "Mrs. Cohen, how you like it here?"

Mrs. Cohen went on and on about the wonderful food, the facility, and the care takers. She said, "But the best thing is that I now have a boyfriend."

Mrs. Murphy said, "Now isn't that wonderful. Tell me all about it."

Mrs. Cohen said, "After lunch we go up to my room and sit on the edge of the bed. I let him touch me on the top, and then on the bottom, and then we sing Jewish songs."

Mrs. Murphy said, "For sure it's a blessing. I am so glad for you."

Mrs. Cohen said, "And how is it with you, Mrs. Murphy?"

Mrs. Murphy said it was also wonderful at her new facility, and that she also had a boyfriend.

Mrs. Cohen said, "Good for you. So what do you do?"

"We also go up to my room after lunch and sit on the edge of the bed. I let him touch me on top, and let him touch me down below."

Mrs. Cohen said, "Yes? And then?"

Mrs. Murphy said, "Since we don't know any songs, we screw."

Lightning Strikes

Two old matronly sisters lived together and managed a farm. All their lives they had both had an extreme fear of thunder storms and lightning.

One day, one of the sisters was visiting a neighbor, and while walking home, she was caught in a severe thunder storm. Lightning was streaking across the sky and thunder was booming all around.

The old woman was completely terrified, ran to a nearby haystack, and buried her head in the hay like an ostrich, so she could not see the lightning or hear the thunder.

With her head buried in the hay, her rear end was exposed to the elements, and the wind blew her dress up exposing a long unused part of her anatomy.

Along came the local stud, and seeing the poor woman's predicament, he did the only thing a well endowed stud would do in such a situation.

After fully satisfying himself he zipped up his pants and went on his merry way.

Soon, the woman pulled her head out of the haystack and rushed home, calling to her sister, "Sister, sister, let me tell you something. I was just hit by lightning and have to tell you that we never should be afraid again.

Remembering Things

A couple in their nineties is having problems remembering things, so they decide to the go the doctor for a checkup. The doctor tells them that they are physically fine, but they might want to start writing things down to help them remember.

Later that night, they are watching TV and the old man gets up from his chair. His wife asks, "Where are you going?"

"To the kitchen," he replies.

She asks, "Will you bring me a bowl of ice cream?"

The husband says, "Sure."

She gently reminds him, "Don't you think you should write it down so you can remember it?"

He says, "No, I can remember that."

She then says, "I would also like some strawberries on top. You better write it down, because I know you will forget it."

He says, "I can remember a bowl of ice cream with strawberries."

She adds, "I also like whipped cream and am certain you will forget that so you better write it down."

He says, "I don't need to write it down. I can remember ice cream with strawberries and whipped cream." He grumbles and goes into the kitchen.

After about twenty minutes the old man returns from the kitchen and hands his wife a plate of bacon and eggs.

She stares at the plate for a moment and says, "Where is my toast?"

Buff at Breakfast

A couple who had been married for fifty years were sitting at the breakfast table one morning when the old gentleman said to his wife, "Just think, honey, we have been married for fifty years."

"Yeah," she replied, "Just think, fifty years ago we were sitting here at this same breakfast table together."

"I know," the old man said, "We were probably sitting here naked as jaybirds fifty years ago."

Granny winked at him and snickered, "What do you think? Should we get naked?"

The two stripped to the buff and sat down at the table.

"You know, honey," the old woman said, "My nipples are as hot for you today as they were fifty years ago."

"I wouldn't be surprised," replied her husband. "One's in your coffee and the other is in your oatmeal."

Rocking Chair

Two elderly residents, a man and a woman, were sitting alone in the lobby of their nursing home one evening.

The old man looked over and said to the old lady, "I know just what you want. For five dollars I'll have sex with you right over there in that rocking chair."

The old lady looked surprised, but didn't say a word.

The old man continued, "For ten dollars I'll do it with you on that nice soft sofa over there, but for twenty dollars I'll take you back to my room, light some candles, and give you the most romantic evening you have ever had in your life."

The old lady still says nothing, but after a couple minutes, starts digging down in her purse. She pulls out a wrinkled twenty dollar bill and holds it up.

"So you want the nice romantic evening in my room," says the old man.

"Get serious," she replies. "I want you to do it to me four times in the rocking chair."

Love on a Cruise

Mr. Smith had been retired for a year when his wife of forty years suggested, "Why don't we take a cruise for a week and make wild passionate love like we did when we were young?"

He thought it over and agreed. He put on his hat and coat and went down to the corner drug store. He stepped up to the counter and asked for a bottle of seasick pills and a box of condoms.

Upon returning home his wife greeted him at the door saying, "You know dear, I have been thinking it over and I see no reason why we can't manage a month long cruise so we could relax and make wild passionate love like we did when we were young."

He smiled, turned around, and went back to the pharmacy. He stepped up and ordered twelve bottles of seasick pills and a dozen boxes of condoms.

Upon returning back home his wife met him on the porch with a big smile on her face.

"Honey, I have a marvelous idea. Now that our children are all on their own, there is nothing to stop us from cruising around the world."

"I'll be right back," he said. Back to the drug store he went. When he approached the pharmacy counter the druggist looked up with a puzzled grin.

The man sheepishly ordered two hundred bottles of seasick pills and the same number of boxes of condoms.

The pharmacist busied himself filling the order then passed the wrapped package across the counter saying, "You know, Mr. Smith, you have been doing business with me for over thirty years. I certainly don't mean to pry, but if it makes you that sick, why do you do it so much?"

Do You Remember

Grandpa and grandpa were sitting in their porch rockers watching the beautiful sunset and reminiscing about the good old days, when grandma turned to grandpa and said, "Honey, do you remember when we first started dating and you used to just casually reach over and take my hand?"

Grandpa looked over at her, smiled, and obligingly took her aged hand in his.

With a smile, grandma pressed a little farther, "Honey, do you remember how after we were engaged, you would sometimes lean over and suddenly kiss me on the cheek?"

Grandpa leaned slowly toward grandma and gave her a lingering kiss on her wrinkled cheek.

Growing bolder still, grandma said, "Honey, do you remember how, after we were first married, you would kind of nibble on my ear?"

Grandpa slowly gets up from his rocker and heads into the house.

Grandma said, "Dear, where are you going?"

Grandpa replied, "To get my teeth."

Granddad

One evening a grandson was talking to his grandfather about current events. The grandson asked his grandfather what he thought about the shootings at schools, the computer age, and just things in general.

The granddad replied, "Well, let me think a minute. I was born before television, penicillin, polio shots, frozen food, Xerox, contact lenses, Frisbees and the pill. There was no radar, credit cards, laser beams, or ballpoint pens.

Man had not invented pantyhose, air conditioners, dishwashers, clothes dryers, and the clothes were hung out to dry in the fresh air, and man had not yet walked on the moon.

Your grandmother and I got married first, and then lived together. Every family had a father and a mother. Until I was twenty five, I called every man older than I, 'Sir' and after I turned twenty five, I still called policemen and every man with a title, 'Sir'.

We were before gay-rights, computer dating, dual careers, daycare centers, and group therapy. Our lives were governed by the Ten Commandments, good judgment, and common sense.

We were taught to know the difference between right and wrong and to stand up and take responsibility for our actions. Serving your country was a privilege.

Having a meaningful relationship meant getting along with your cousins. Time-sharing meant time the family spent together in the evenings and weekends not purchasing condominiums.

We never heard of FM radios, tape decks, CDs, yogurt, or guys wearing earrings. We listened to Jack Benny, and the President's speeches on our radios. If you saw anything with 'Made in Japan' on it, it was junk. Pizza Hut, McDonald's, and instant coffee were unheard of.

We had 5 and 10 cent stores where you could actually buy things for 5 and 10 cents. Ice cream cones, phone calls, rides on a streetcar, and a Pepsi were all a nickel. If you didn't want to splurge, you could spend your nickel on enough stamps to mail one letter and two postcards.

You could buy a new Chevy Coupe for $600, but who could afford one? Gas was eleven cents a gallon.

In my day, 'grass' was mowed, 'coke' was a cold drink, 'pot' was something your mother cooked in, and 'rock music' was your grandmother's lullaby.

'Aids' were helpers in the Principal's office, 'chip' meant a piece of wood, hardware was found in a hardware store, and software wasn't even a word.

We were the last generation to actually believe that a lady needed a husband to have a baby.

No wonder people call us old and confused and say there is a generation gap.

How old do you think I am?"

The man would be only 65.

Forgiveness

Sunday's sermon was titled, "Forgive Your Enemies."

Toward the end of the service the minister asked, "How many of you have forgiven your enemies?"

Most of the congregation held up their hands.

He repeated the question, and this time everyone responded except for one small, elderly lady.

"Mrs. Jones? Are you not willing to forgive your enemies?"

"I don't have any enemies," she responded sweetly.

"Mrs. Jones, that's very unusual. How old are you?"

"Ninety-eight," was the reply.

"Oh, Mrs. Jones, would you please come down to the front and tell us all how a person can live to be ninety-eight and not have an enemy in the world?"

This sweetheart of an old lady tottered down the aisle, faced the congregation with a grin on her face and said, "I outlived all the old bitches."

Oldie is a Goodie

An old man turned 115 and was being interviewed by a reporter for the local paper. During the interview the reporter noticed that the yard was full of children of all ages playing together. A very pretty girl served the old man and the reporter, keeping them in fresh tea and running errands for them.

"Are these your grandkids?" the reporter asked.

"Naw, sir, they all be my young 'uns," the old man replied with a grin.

"Your kids?" said the reporter. "What about this beautiful young lady who keeps bringing us tea? Is she one of your children too?"

"Naw, sir," said the old man. "She be my wife."

"Your wife?" said the surprised reporter, "But she can't be more than 19 years old."

"Thass right," said the old man with pride.

"Well, surely you can't have a sex life with you being 115 and she being only 19," the reporter remarked.

"Sir," said the old man. "We have sex every night. Every night two of my boys helps me on it, and every morning six of my boys helps me off."

"Wait just a minute," said the newspaperman. "Why does it only take two of your boys to put you on, but it takes six of them to take you off?"

"Cuz," the spry old man said with a balled fist, "I fights 'em."

Ailments

A group of seniors were sitting around their nursing home parlor talking about all their ailments. "My arms have become so weak I can hardly lift this cup of coffee," said one.

"Yes, I know," said another. "My cataracts are so bad I can't even see my coffee."

"I couldn't even mark an 'X' at election time, my hands are so crippled," volunteered a third.

"What, speak up, what, I can't hear you," said a fourth.

"I can't turn my head because of the arthritis in my neck," said a fifth, to which several nodded weakly in agreement.

"My blood pressure pills make me so dizzy I can hardly walk," exclaimed another.

"I forget where I am, and where I'm going," said another elderly gent.

"I guess that's the price we pay for getting old," winced an old man as he slowly shook his head. The others nodded in agreement.

"Well, count your blessings," said one woman cheerfully, "Thankfully, we can all still drive."

Grandpa's Wisdom

Whether a man winds up with a nest egg, or a goose egg, depends a lot on the kind of chick he marries.

Trouble in marriage often starts when a man gets so busy earnin' his salt, that he forgets his sugar.

Too many couples marry for better, or for worse, but not for good.

If a man has enough horse sense to treat his wife like a thoroughbred, she will never turn into an old nag.

On anniversaries, the wise husband always forgets the past, but never the present.

The bonds of matrimony are a good investment, only when the interest is kept up.

Many girls like to marry a military man - he can cook, sew, make beds, is in good health, and he is already used to taking orders.

Eventually you will reach a point when you stop lying about your age, and start bragging about it.

The older we get, the fewer things seem worth waiting in line for.

How old would you be if you didn't know how old you are?

When you are dissatisfied and would like to go back to your youth, remember about Algebra.

One of the many things no one tells you about aging is that it is such a nice change from being young.

Ah, being young is beautiful, but being old is comfortable.

Old age is when former classmates are so gray and wrinkled and bald, they don't recognize you.

Viagra Works

Man goes to visit his eighty-five-year-old grandpa in hospital. "How are you grandpa?" he asks.

"Feeling fine," says the old man.

"What's the food like?"

"Terrific, wonderful food."

"And the nursing?"

"Just couldn't be better. These young nurses really take care of you."

"What about sleeping? Do you sleep OK?"

"No problem at all, nine hours solid every night. At ten o'clock they bring me a cup of hot chocolate and a Viagra tablet, and that's it. I go out like a light."

The grandson is puzzled and a little alarmed by this, so rushes off to question the nurse in charge. "What are you people doing," he says, "I'm told you are giving an eighty-five-year-old Viagra on a daily basis. Surely that can't be true?"

"Oh, yes," replies the nurse. "Every night at ten o'clock we give him a cup of chocolate and a Viagra tablet. It works wonderfully well. The chocolate makes him sleep and the Viagra stops him rolling out of bed."

Longevity

An eighty year old man went to the doctor for a checkup and the doctor was amazed at what good shape the guy was in. The doctor asked, "To what do you attribute your good health?"

The old timer said, "I'm a golfer. That's why I am in such good shape. I get up before daylight and go out golfing."

The doctor said, "I am sure that helps, but there has to be more to it. How old was your dad when he died?"

The old timer said, "Who said my dad's dead?"

The doctor said, "You mean you are eighty years old and your dad is still alive? How old is he?"

The old timer said, "He's a hundred, and he golfed with me this morning, and that's why he is still alive, He's also a golfer."

The doctor said, "How about your dad's dad? How old was he when he died?"

The old timer said, "Who said my grandpa's dead?"

The doctor said, "Wow, how old is your grandfather?"

The old timer said, "He's a hundred and eighteen years old."

The doctor said, "I guess he went golfing with you this morning too?"

The old timer said, "No, grandpa couldn't go this morning, because he just got married."

The doctor said in amazement, "Got married. Why would a hundred and eighteen year old guy want to get married?"

The old timer said, "Who said he wanted to?"

Fairy Grandmother

A couple had been married for fifty years and was celebrating their seventieth birthdays together.

During the celebration a fairy grandmother appeared and said that because they had been such a loving couple all those years, she would give them one wish each.

Being the faithful, loving spouse for all these years, the husband wanted for them both to have a romantic vacation together, so he wished for them to travel around the world.

The fairy grandmother waved her wand.

POOF! He had the tickets in his hand.

Next, it was the wife's turn and the fairy grandmother assured her she could have any wish she wanted, all he needed to do was ask for her heart's desire.

She paused for a moment, and then said, "To be honest, I would like to have a man thirty years younger than I am so he could keep up with my desires."

The fairy picked up her wand.

POOF!

She was a hundred.

Nothing Too Strenuous

On hearing that her elderly grandfather had just passed away, a woman went straight to her grandparent's house to visit her ninety year old grandmother and comfort her.

When she asked how her grandfather had died, her grandmother replied, "He had a heart attack while we were making love on Sunday morning."

She was horrified and told her grandmother that two people nearly ninety years old having sex would surely be asking for trouble.

"Oh no, my dear," replied her granny. "Many years ago, we realized our advanced age, and we figured out the best time to do it was when the church bells would start to ring. It was just the right rhythm. Nice and slow and even. Nothing too strenuous, simply do it in on the ding and out on the dong."

She paused, wiped away a tear, and then continued, "If that damned ice cream truck hadn't come along, he would still be alive today."

Granddad Golf

A father, son, and grandson go out to the country club for their weekly round of golf. Just as they reach the first tee, a beautiful young blonde woman carrying her bag of clubs approaches them. She explains that the member who brought her to the club for a round of golf had an emergency, was called away, and asks the trio whether she can join them.

Naturally, the guys all agree. The blonde thanks them and says, "Look, fellows, I work in a topless bar as a dancer, so nothing shocks me anymore. If any of you wants to smoke cigars, have a beer, bet, swear or tell off-color stories or do anything that you normally do when playing a round together, go ahead.

I enjoy playing golf and consider myself pretty good at it, so don't try to coach me on how to play my shots."

With that the guys agree to relax and invite her to drive first. All eyes are fastened on her shapely behind as she bends to place her ball on the tee. She then takes her driver and hits the ball 270 yards down the middle, right in front of the green.

"That was beautiful," said the dad. The blonde puts her driver away and says, "I really didn't get into it, and I should have faded it a little."

After the three guys hit their drives and their second shots the blonde takes out a nine iron and lofts the ball within three feet of the hole.

The son says, "Dang, lady, you played that perfectly."

The blonde frowns and says, "It was a little weak. I left a tricky little putt."

After the son buries a long putt for a par, dad two putts for a bogey and granddad overruns the green with his pitching wedge, chips back, and putts for a double bogey, the blonde taps in the three-footer for a birdie.

The guys all congratulate her on her fine game. She puts her putter back in the bag and says, "Thanks, but I really haven't played much lately, and I'm a little rusty. Maybe I will really get into this next drive."

Having the honors, she drives first on the second hole and knocks the heck out of the ball, and it lands nearly 300 yards away, smack in the middle of the fairway. For the rest of the round the statuesque blonde continues to amaze the guys, quietly and methodically shooting for par or less on every hole.

When they get to the 18th green, the blonde is three under par, but has a very nasty 12-foot putt on an undulating green for a par. She turns to the three guys and says, "I really want to thank you all for not acting like a bunch of chauvinists and telling me what club to use or how to play a shot, but I need this putt for a 69 and I would really like to break 70 on this course. If any one of you can tell me how to make par on this hole, I will take him back to my apartment, pour some 25-year old Scotch in him, fix him dinner, and then show him a good time the rest of the night."

The yuppie son jumps at the thought. He strolls across the green, carefully eyes the line of the putt, and finally says, "Honey, aim about six inches to the right of the hole and hit it firm. It will get over that little hump and break into the cup."

The father kneels down and sights the putt using his putter as a plumb. "Don't listen to the kid, you want to hit it softly ten inches to the right and run it left down that little hogback, so it falls into the cup."

The old gray haired grandfather walks over to the blonde's ball on the green, picks it up, and hands it to her.

"That's a gimme, sweetheart. Your car or mine?"

Grandma's Birthday

The family wheeled grandma out on the lawn in her wheelchair, where the activities for her hundredth birthday were taking place.

Grandma couldn't speak very well, but she could write notes when she needed to communicate.

After a short time out on the lawn, grandma started leaning off to the right, so some family members grabbed her, straightened her up, and stuffed pillows on her right.

A short time later, she started leaning off to her left, so again the family grabbed her and stuffed pillows on her left.

Soon she started leaning forward, so the family members again grabbed her, and then tied a pillowcase around her waist to hold her up.

A nephew who arrived late came running up to grandma and said, "Hi grandma, you are looking good. How are they treating you?"

Grandma took out her notepad and wrote a note to the nephew, "Fine, but I wish they would just let me fart once in a while."

Older Women

- An older woman will never wake you in the middle of the night to ask, "What are you thinking?" She does not care what you think.

- An older woman knows herself well enough to be assured in who she is, what she is, what she wants, and from whom. Few women past the age of 50 give a damn what you might think about them.

- Older women are dignified. They seldom have a screaming match with you in the middle of an expensive restaurant. Of course, if you deserve it, they won't hesitate to shoot you if they think they can get away with it.

- Most older women cook well, care about cleanliness, and are generous with praise.

- An older woman has the self-assurance to introduce you to her women friends. A younger woman with a man will often ignore even her best friend, because she doesn't trust the guy with other women.

- Women get psychic as they age. You never have to confess your sins to an older woman. They always know.

- An older woman looks good wearing bright red lipstick. This is not true of younger women or drag queens.

- Once you get past a wrinkle or two, an older woman is far sexier than her younger counterpart. Her libido is stronger and her fear of pregnancy is gone. Her experience in lovemaking is honed and reciprocal. She has lived long enough to know how to please a man in ways her daughter could never dream of.

- Older women are forthright and honest. They will tell you that you are a jerk, if you are acting like one.

Advice from Old People

Forget looks an' boobs an' crap. All ya needs from life is a woman with a heart of gold and a fanny like a jar of worms.

People in power only hold that power, because you allow them to. If they abuse that power, you can take it away from them. This applies to employers, landlords, governments, and especially relationships.

It is easier to get a girlfriend when you already have a girlfriend.

Remember to screw around a lot, when we were growing up we were not allowed to.

Never look at your mom when she is eating a banana.

Learn this important lesson on dealing with a wife. If you are going out for a night on the town, tell her you are coming home an hour or two later than you actually intend to. That way, when you arrive home early she will be delighted that you have cut short your night out to be with her.

Never chase after a bus or a girl - another one will come along soon enough.

Advice from a granddad - Don't listen to your mother, she never has known what she is talking about.

Don't tell a diabetic that a spoonful of sugar helps the medicine go down.

Ugly women have vaginas too.

Never sleep with a woman whose problems are worse than your own.

Women are like cow pies, the older they are, the easier they are to pick up.

Passing On

Agonies

An elderly Italian man lay dying in his bed, suffering the agonies of impending death. He suddenly smelled the aroma of his favorite Italian anisette sprinkle cookies wafting up the stairs.

He gathered his remaining strength, and lifted himself from the bed. Leaning against the wall, he slowly made his way out of the bedroom and crawled downstairs. With labored breath, he leaned against the doorframe, gazing into the kitchen.

Were it not for death's agony, he would have thought himself already in heaven, for there, spread out upon waxed paper on the kitchen table were literally hundreds of his favorite anisette sprinkle cookies.

Was it heaven, or was it one final act of heroic love from his devoted Italian wife of sixty years, seeing to it that he left this world a happy man?

Mustering one great final effort, he threw himself towards the table, landing on his knees in a rumpled posture. His parched lips parted, the wondrous taste of the cookie was already in his mouth, seemingly bringing him back to life.

The aged and withered hand trembled on its way to a cookie at the edge of the table, when it was suddenly smacked with a spatula by his wife.

"Back off, those are for the funeral," she said.

Memorial Stone

A woman's husband died. All he had was twenty thousand dollars to leave behind for his wife.

After paying all the funeral expenses, she told her closest friend that there was no money left.

The friend asked, "How can that be? You told me he had twenty thousand dollars a few days before he died. How could you be broke so quickly?"

The widow replied, "The funeral cost me six thousand five hundred dollars.

Of course, I had to make the obligatory donation to the church to pay for the organist and services.

I gave five hundred dollars to the priest, and I spent another five hundred bucks for the wake, the food, and drinks.

The rest went for the memorial stone."

The friend said, "Twelve thousand five hundred dollars for the memorial stone? My God, how big was it?"

The widow replied, "Three carats."

Finally Together

Maria is a devout Catholic. She gets married and together with her husband, they have fifteen children.

Soon after the fifteenth child is born her husband dies.

A few months later she remarries and during the following years has another ten children with her second husband.

After the tenth child is born her second husband dies.

Within a month Maria is engaged to be married a third time. Unfortunately, she becomes very ill and dies.

At her wake, the priest looks tenderly at Maria as she lies in her coffin. He looks up to the heavens and says, "At least, they are finally together."

A man standing next to the priest asks, "Excuse me Father, but do you mean Maria and her first husband, or Maria and her second husband?"

The priest says, "I mean her legs."

Burial

John went on a vacation to the Middle East with his family including his mother-in-law. During their vacation in Jerusalem, John's mother-in-law died.

With the death certificate in his hand, John went to the American Consulate Office to make arrangements to send the body back to the United States for a proper burial.

The Consul told him that to send the body back to the United States for burial was very, very expensive. It could cost, him as much as five thousand dollars.

The Consul added that, in most cases the person responsible for the remains normally decides to bury the body here in Jerusalem. This would only cost him about two hundred dollars American.

John thought for sometime and said, "I don't care how much it will cost to send the body back. That is what I want to do."

The Consul replied "You must have loved your mother-in-law very much considering the difference in price."

"No, it's not that," said John. "You see, I heard of a case a long time ago of a man that was buried here in Jerusalem. On the third day he arose from the dead, and I just can't take that chance with my mother-in-law"

That Damn Wall

A funeral service is being held for a woman who has just passed away. At the end of the service the pallbearers are carrying the casket out when they accidentally bump into a wall, jarring the casket.

They hear a faint moan. They open the casket and find that the woman is actually alive. She lives for ten more years, and then finally dies.

A ceremony is again held at the same place, and at the end of the ceremony the pallbearers are again carrying out the casket.

As they are walking, the husband cries out, "Watch out for the damn wall."

Heaven

A ninety year old couple had been married almost sixty years and died in a car crash. They had been in good health the last ten years, mainly due to her interest in health food and exercise.

When they reached the Pearly Gates, Saint Peter took them to their mansion which was decked out with a beautiful kitchen, master bath suite, and Jacuzzi.

As they looked around in wonder, the old man asked Peter how much all this would cost.

"It is all free," Peter replied. "This is Heaven."

Next, they went out back to see the championship golf course that the home backed up to. They would have golfing privileges everyday and each week the course changed to a new one representing the great golf courses on Earth.

The old man asked, "What are the green fees?"

Peter's reply, "This is Heaven, you play for free."

Next they went to the club house and saw the lavish buffet lunch with the cuisines of the world laid out.

"How much to eat?" asked the old man.

This is Heaven, it is free." Peter replied.

"Where are the low fat and low cholesterol foods?"

Peter explained, "That's the best part, you can eat as much as you like of whatever you like and you never get fat and you never get sick. This is Heaven."

The old man looked at his wife and said, "You and your stupid bran muffins. I could have been here ten years ago."

Empty Seat

John managed to snag fifty-yard line tickets for the Super Bowl. As he sits down, Paul comes down the row and asks if anyone is sitting in the seat next to him.

"No," John says. "The seat is empty."

"This is incredible," says Paul.

"Who in their right mind would have a seat like this for the Super Bowl, the biggest sporting event in the world, and not use it?"

John says, "Actually, the seat belongs to me. I was supposed to come with my wife, but she passed away. This is the first Super Bowl we haven't been to together since we were married fifteen years ago."

"Oh, I am sorry to hear that. That's terrible. Couldn't you find someone else, like a friend or relative, or even a neighbor to take the seat?"

John shakes his head, "No, they are all at the funeral."

Take it With You

A man worked hard all of his life and saved his money. In fact, he loved money so much that just before he died, he asked his wife to put the money in the casket with him, because he wanted to take it with him to the afterlife.

His wife made a solemn promise and said, "Sure, I will put all of the money in the casket."

The day of his death arrived. He was stretched out in the casket. The wife was sitting there in black and her friend was sitting next to her.

When they finished the ceremony, just before the undertakers got ready to close the casket, the wife said, "Wait." She had a box with her, went over to the casket and put the box in.

The undertakers locked the casket lid down, and they rolled it away.

Her friend was amazed and said, "You weren't fool enough to put all that money in there?"

The widow replied, "I am a Christian, I can't lie. I promised him solemnly that I would put the money in that casket."

"All of it?"

The wife said, "Sure, I wrote him a check for the full amount."

The Card Game

Six retired Floridians were playing poker in the condo clubhouse when Meyers loses five hundred dollars on a single hand, clutches his chest, and drops dead at the table.

Showing respect for their fallen comrade, the other five continue to play standing up.

Finkelstein looks around and asks, "So, who should tell his wife?"

They draw cards and Goldberg picks the lowest one.

They tell him to be discreet and gentle, and to not make a bad situation any worse.

"Discreet? I am the most discreet person you will ever meet. Discretion is my middle name. Leave it to me."

Goldberg goes over to the Meyers' apartment and knocks on the door.

The wife answers and asks what he wants. Goldberg declares, "Your husband just lost five hundred dollars playing cards, and is afraid to come home."

"Tell him to drop dead," says the wife.

"I'll go tell him," says Goldberg.

Mourning

A man placed some flowers on the grave of his dearly departed mother and started back toward his car when his attention was diverted to another man kneeling at a grave.

The man seemed to be praying with profound intensity and kept repeating, "Why did you have to die? Why did you have to die?"

The first man approached him and said, "Sir, I don't wish to intrude on your private grief, but this demonstration of pain is more than I have ever seen before. For whom do you mourn so deeply? A child? A parent?"

The mourner took a moment to collect himself, then replied, "My wife's first husband."

Funeral Procession

A man was leaving the store with his morning coffee when he noticed a most unusual funeral procession approaching the nearby cemetery. A long black hearse was followed by a second long black hearse about fifty feet behind.

Behind the second hearse was a solitary man walking a pit bull dog on a leash. Behind, were two hundred men walking single file.

The man couldn't stand the curiosity. He respectfully approached the man walking the dog and said, "I am so sorry for your loss, and I know now is a bad time to disturb you, but I have never seen a funeral like this. Whose funeral is it?"

The man replied, "Well, that first hearse is for my wife"

"What happened to her?"

The man replied, "My dog attacked and killed her."

He inquired further, "Who is in the second hearse?"

The man answered, "My mother-in-law. She was trying to help my wife when the dog turned on her."

A poignant and thoughtful moment of silence passes between the two men.

"May I borrow the dog?"

"Get in line."

Spelling

After a long illness, a woman died and arrived at the Gates of Heaven. While she was waiting, she peeked through the Gates and saw a beautiful banquet table. Sitting all around were her parents and all the other people she had loved and who had died before her.

They saw her and began calling greetings to her, "Hello, how are you? We have been waiting for you. Good to see you."

When Saint Peter came by, the woman said to him, "This is such a wonderful place. How do I get in?"

"You have to spell a word," Saint Peter told her.

"Which word?" the woman asked.

"Love."

The woman correctly spelled 'L o v e' and Saint Peter welcomed her into Heaven.

About six months later, Saint Peter came to the woman and asked her to watch the Gates of Heaven for him that day.

While the woman was guarding the Pearly Gates, her husband arrived. She said, "I am surprised to see you. How have you been?"

"I have been doing well since you died. I married the beautiful young nurse who took care of you while you were ill. Then I won the lottery and sold the little house we lived in and bought a big mansion. My new wife and I traveled all around the world. I went water skiing today, fell, hit my head, and here I am. How do I get in?"

"You have to spell a word," the woman told him.

"Which word?" her husband asked.

"Czechoslovakia."

337

Life after Death

A couple made a deal that whoever died first would come back and inform the other of the after life. The woman's biggest fear was that there was no heaven. After a long life the husband was the first to go and true to his word he made contact.

"Mary, Mary."

"Is that you Fred?"

"Yes, I have come back like we agreed."

"What is it like?"

"Well, I get up in the morning, I have sex, I have breakfast, I have sex. I bathe in the sun, and then I have sex-twice. I have lunch, then sex pretty much all afternoon. After supper more sex until late at night, then sleep and start all over again."

"Oh Fred you surely must be in heaven."

"Heck no. I came back as a rabbit."

Mary Clancy

Father O'Grady was saying his good-byes to the parishioners after his Sunday morning service as he always does. Just then Mary Clancy came up to him in tears.

"What's bothering you so, dear?" inquired Father O'Grady.

"Oh, father, I have terrible news," replied Mary.

"Well what is it, Mary?"

"My husband, passed away last night, Father."

"Oh, Mary" said the priest, "That is terrible.

Tell me Mary, did he have any last requests?"

"Well, yes he did father," replied Mary.

"What did he ask, Mary?"

Mary replied, "He told me to please put the gun down."

Ashes

Georgia recently lost her husband. She had him cremated and brought his ashes home.

Picking up the urn that he was in, she poured him out on the patio table. Then, while tracing her fingers in the ashes, she started talking to him.

"Herman, you know that fur coat you promised me? I bought it with the insurance money."

She paused for a minute tracing her fingers in the ashes then said, "Herman, remember that new car you promised me? I also bought it with the insurance money."

Again, she paused for a few minutes and while tracing her fingers in the ashes she said, "Herman, that emerald necklace you promised me, I bought it too, with the insurance money."

Finally, still tracing her fingers in the ashes, she said, "Herman, remember that blow job I promised you?"

"Here it comes."

To be happy with a man,
you must understand him a lot and love him a little.

To be happy with a woman,
you must love her a lot and not try to understand her
at all.